Signs of Borges

A Book in the Series

Latin America in Translation/En Traducción/Em Tradução

Sponsored by the Duke–University of North Carolina

Joint Program in Latin Ameı

D1205197

Post-Contemporary Interventions

Series Editors:

Stanley Fish

and

Fredric Jameson

Sylvia Molloy

Signs

of

Borges

Translated and Adapted

by Oscar Montero

in Collaboration with

the Author

Thomas J. Bata Library
TRENT UNIVERSITY
WITHDRAWN
PETERBOROUGH, ONTARIO

Duke University Press   Durham and London

1994

PQ7797.B635 Z78413
,1994

Translation of the books in the series Latin America in Translation/En Traducción/Em Tradução, a collaboration between the Duke–University of North Carolina Joint Program in Latin American Studies and the university presses of Duke and the University of North Carolina, is supported by a grant from the Andrew W. Mellon Foundation.

© 1994 Duke University Press
All rights reserved
Printed in the United States
of America on acid-free paper ∞
Designed by Cherie Holma Westmoreland
Typeset in Meridien with Trajanus display
by Keystone Typesetting, Inc.

*Library of Congress Cataloging-in-
Publication Data*

Molloy, Sylvia. [Letras de Borges. English] Signs of
Borges / Sylvia Molloy ; translated and adapted by Oscar
Montero in collaboration with the Author. p. cm. —
(Post-contemporary interventions) (Latin America in trans-
lation/en traducción/em tradução) Includes index.
ISBN 0-8223-1406-1. — ISBN 0-8223-1420-7 (pbk)
1. Borges, Jorge Luis, 1899– —Criticism and interpretation. I. Montero, Oscar, 1947– . II. Title. III. Series.
IV. Series: Latin America in translation/en traducción/em
tradução.   PQ7797.B635Z78413   1994   868—dc20
93-11260 CIP

For María Luisa Bastos
who, years ago, told me to
read Borges

Contents

Preface

Any attempt to reconstruct the steps that led me, more than fifteen years ago, to write this particular book on Borges and not another would be illusory. I would like to think that my reflections on reading Borges may have been of use to others then, as they were to me. Borges taught me to think about literature, even to write it. *Las letras de Borges* wanted to acknowledge that debt.

I speak casually of *this* book as if it had not changed, even when I realize that, by now, it is no longer the same. The book I wrote in Spanish, as an explication and an homage, is now, in its English version, another book, unfamiliar, a little disquieting. I have contributed to its translation willingly yet not without trepidation, reading it with other eyes, conversing with it at every turn. It is, to quote the title of one of Borges's books of poems, *el otro, el mismo.* It is a book in which I recognize myself fully; it is also a book that I might not have written today.

New York, 1993

Signs of Borges

His features had become familiar to me, charged with a meaning that was of no importance but none the less intelligible like a script which one can read, and had ceased in any way to resemble those strange and repellent characteristics which his face had presented to me on that first day.

Marcel Proust,
Within a Budding Grove

Introduction

To read Borges, to consume a predictable Borges who no longer surprises us, has become a habit. By common accord, it would seem, readers of Borges, with the collaboration perhaps of the author himself, have turned an unstable text into a solid monument. What was fragmentary has become stable; critical inquiry, a mere habit.

Borges is consumed voraciously. The marks that break the flow of the text and hint at its uncanniness are hastily incorporated, in the crudest sense: in order to get rid of them as quickly as possible. The physical metaphor is not entirely impertinent, underscoring a voracity that no longer recognizes its true appetite. Like bodies, readers have become mere passages for the text and have learned to ignore a critical summons that urges them to read differently.

To undo the habit, to dwell on the text, as one would pause before what one is about to incorporate, foreseeing pleasure but also, disquietingly, intuiting strangeness: isn't that what reading is about? Borges's text is not hospitable; at first, we have trouble just staying with its initial rejection and our initial distrust, trouble recognizing, perhaps, our own hostility. The promise of a flowing text, a text mimicking smoothness, a text that just carries us along (perhaps the most dangerous), gives rise to bad habits. We want texts to pass through us instead of allowing ourselves to grope through the text, stumbling against unwieldy fragments, aware of and puzzled by our discomfort.

My use of the first person plural is questionable. It is obvious that the fragments that disturb one reader will do nothing for another. It is also obvious that those unsettling fragments are, as literature is for Borges, moveable elements that in other times, or for other readers, will not necessarily be disturbing in the same way. The gaps, the ambiguities, the quirks on which I dwell today may well not be those at which a future reader stops, or even one of my contemporaries. It is hard to turn shock into a common experience. To do so would trivialize all breaks, or at least institutionalize them, thus impoverishing our perception of them.

I propose the following working hypothesis, not new to be sure; that for different reasons, Borges's text disturbs some readers, among whom I count myself, and that the disquiet produced by that text is of a peculiar nature. Borges is one more example of an author whose potential for disquiet, or better still, whose intellectual provocation, has been weakened by a tradition of reductive readings. Like Kafka, Beckett, or Nabokov, his name has been domesticated, has become a mere password. For instance, the expressions *Borgesian* or *Kafkaesque* are no longer denotative. They are connotative, to be sure, but their connotation is limited: everyone *knows* what they mean.

In order to approach what is unsettling, or uncanny, in Borges, I choose to follow his text's shifting perspective, its vocation, one might say, for nonfixity, accompanied by its tenuous longing for what is fixed. Borges's oscillation between fixity and mobility reproduces the oscillation between "the nothingness of personality," to quote the title of one of his early essays, and the obvious self-centeredness that shapes his early poetry. However, even then, and in spite of the explicit solipsism of these early poems, Borges *passes through* his texts. Already in those texts there is fragmentation, a shifting and shifty *persona* writing up its fissures, its hesitation.

The early poetry by Borges, as well as his first critical texts, for example, the essays from *Inquisiciones, El tamaño de mi esperanza,* and *El idioma de los argentinos*, no doubt announce the deliberately transient character of Borges's text. Yet the full implications of his wavering discourse, of his textual probing, only becomes obvious (and therefore a subject of discussion), when Borges begins to write his fictions. Curiously, critics have latched on to that least defined of genres to justify their condemnation or their praise of Borges. My point of departure is no different from that of those critics, although exempt, I hope, from mere praise or condemnation. Borges's fictions are not basically different from the rest of Borges's work; they afford, however, a choice vantage point from which to observe the whole work.

In this book I consider Borges's narrative texts for what they are, a collection of stories, and at the same time, I point out what connects them, from their unsettling beginnings on, to the rest of his work. I wish to describe the attitude that shapes Borges's fictions or early protofictions, a mixture of parodic exaggeration and doubtful erudition in *A Universal History of Infamy* and a consciously crafted nostalgia in *Evaristo Carriego*. From those first narrative exercises, this book details Borges's play of masks, the shift from the personal, almost regional, level of the early biography of Carriego, to the carnivalesque, clearly exotic, "infamous biographies," and then on (Borges having almost didactically prepared the reader) to a plural textual masking, organized as "gradual deceptions." In *Signs of Borges* I also wish to note Borges's pleasure in deviating from the simplest rules of the narrative game: his exploration (and ultimate devastation) of the notion of character; the multiple, discordant projections of his plots; the falsely reassuring order of his enumerations and his series; the tension—desire and repulsion—among the elements of these shattered texts. Finally, on the basis of this inquiry, this book describes, approximately, and respecting the vocation for marginality that moves these texts, the nature of Borges's discourse.

Borges's curious fictions, curious in both a passive and an active sense, do not really differ from the rest of his work. To be sure, they have become emblematic of "Borges" because their break with convention appears more showy and easier to detect than in the other texts. Fiction is always a flashy place. On the other hand, the efficacy of these stories exposes them to the worst risk: that they be considered, as indeed they have been, as the product of game-playing, as merely aesthetic tricks. Such frivolity should be amended, in order to restate the issue in other words, in order to restore to these texts the disquiet within the game, the transformation behind the trick, the irritation caused by the playful, incessant exchange of fragments. Borges's fiction is literally alienating, defying classification. Generic crisscrossings hybridize Borges's text: a fundamental textual restlessness prevails.

Any reading of Borges should take into account the ethics that sustains it. For certain readers, the term might seem strange, even dubious. By ethics I mean the honest conduct and conveyance of a text, seemingly deceitful yet aware of its deceptions, admitting to its inevitable traps, confessing to the creation of simulacra it does nothing to conceal. If a return to Borges, to his entire text, is worthwhile, it is because that text upholds a constant and honest disquisition on writing, his own writing, the writing of others. The signs of Borges question and question again, never arriving at a fixed answer, recognizing their inevitable tautology, their treacherous nature, knowing that they are vainly adding "one more thing" yet not ready to abandon the search: the search for the already written. Like few other writers, Borges recognizes that "literature is the art that knows how to prophesize the time in which it will be silent, that knows how to be angry at its own virtues and to love its own dissolution and court its own end." In spite of that lucid, if disenchanted, assessment, he seeks to accumulate signs that are perhaps dispensable and to carry on an exercise that is perhaps useless. Borges's text upholds, with pride and resignation, the excess of a sign that, at each stage, constitutes a challenge, allows for a difference that opens up, ever so fleetingly, the precarious space of the word.

1

Shadow Plays

To scrawl a brief plot in the ruins of a mask factory.

Jorge Luis Borges, "The Lottery in Babylon"

A Double Mistrust

Borges, unlike Plotinus, did not mind sitting for his portrait. Perhaps he could barely make out the blurred features of that *other* image that was his own. Perhaps he was unaware of them; or perhaps he considered that dwelling on the *disjecta membra* that made up his image was, like the detailed descriptions he condemned in certain authors, an aesthetic mistake. Perhaps, in order to see himself in that fixed visage, he accepted the possibility of inverting the terms of the epilogue to *Dreamtigers*: instead of discovering that the patient labyrinth of lines that he had traced coincided with his one and only face, he might discover that his face, which he could only see reflected in the mirror, was an image, the starting point of a careful narrative strategy.

"It is enough to be forced to drag around this simulacrum in which nature has imprisoned me. Should I further consent to the perpetuation of the image of this image?" (OI 60).[1] Borges consents to a portrait of Borges, but he knows, like Plotinus whom he quotes with special emphasis, that, at the very moment it is fixed, such a portrait becomes a reflection. It is the simulacrum of a perpetually moving entity, an ineffective emblem, a coin whose sides never entirely coincide; it is a yearning for a face or a sign that dissolves the moment someone attempts to inscribe it.

Borges's text works assiduously against fixed images, monstrous images that have been classified, images that are monstrous *because* they have been classified. As such, they do not differ from the pieces that, for Borges, make up "the terrible, immobile museum of Platonic archetypes" (HE 16). Borges's text tries to ignore that fixity—which, because of its imperfection, merely emphasizes the illusion of all classification—and at the same time it hints at the possibility of movement behind the rigidity of simulacra. Indeed, the same terrible, immobile forms are seen as "vivid, powerful and organic" (HE 9) in a second reading of Plato. Summoned and discarded in texts, decried by Borges and at the same time courted by him, so certain is he of the tension that energizes it, the simulacrum, for Borges, may be a metaphor, a character, a plot, literature, an author. It also may be Borges, it also may be the self: "My life is a flight, and I lose everything, and everything belongs to oblivion, or to the other" (L 247).

A double mistrust upholds the *nowhere* of the Borges corpus. A mistrust of immobility (the fixed simulacrum, the mask replacing the living face), it is also mistrust of movement, of the mobile face that only becomes a mask when named. Early in his work, Borges manifests skepticism before that illusory duality, that occlusive duplicity marking the starting point of so many of his stories: "These shifts of identity (as distressing as a masquerade, in which one is not quite certain who is who) omit the real name—presuming there is such a thing as a real name" (UHI 53).

Literature, as conceived and put into practice by Borges, does not differ from that game of plural faces and plural masks. Superimposed texts taint the narratives in which they are inserted; simple words, revitalized in new sequences, seem to question each other. Like those faces and masks, they both harmonize and diverge, in a deliberate, fecund juxtaposition. When discussing the *Thousand and One Nights*, Borges recognizes in Scheherazade's tales the same duplicity, the same uncertainty, the same playful possibility of exchange and dialogue, that he attributes to the play between a face and its questionable replica. He observes that in the telling of the *Thousand and One Nights*, "the antechambers blend with the mirrors; the mask is beneath the face; no longer does anyone know which is the real man and which are his idols" (HE 133).

Borges's work is grounded on that mistrust, on that uncertainty. It is a fecund mistrust of the arbitrary, apparently fixed sign, and its reverse, the no less arbitrary and equally fixed metaphor; a mistrust of the elusive face and its wavering mask—the terms are reversible. The confusion of these partial illusions, so clearly intended and adopted by Borges, has nevertheless baffled critics. Thus, for example, the charges of insubstantiality—that is, of lack of "reality"—brought against his fiction: his stories fall short because they lack *something*. Borges is criticized because "he constructs stories in which ghosts inhabiting geometric spaces or libraries or labyrinths live and suffer in word only."[2] The comment is of course sound since any fiction, any world, any character in a narrative exists *in word only*. It is intended, however, as a reproach. The absence of realistic mimesis baffles critics; the impossibility of linking a vague extratextual reality with a fixed personal element, a round character that would root that reality in the written letter making it "come alive," causes irritation, an irritation far removed from the fruitful irritation that Borges's work generally propounds.

"A Detailed Web of Theories to Validate the Task" (I 32)

The most detailed weaving of theories concerning character in Borges, and no doubt the most didactic, may be found in the essay on Nathaniel Hawthorne. Borges suggests that Hawthorne "first imagined, perhaps unwittingly, a situation, and then sought the characters to embody it" (OI 53). Such a method, adds Borges, "can produce, or tolerate, admirable stories because their brevity makes the plot more visible than the actors" (OI 53).

Borges uses Hawthorne's "Wakefield" as an example. Let us suppose, as Borges does, that Hawthorne's starting point is indeed a narrative situation: a man leaves home to play a trick on his wife and, once outside, is incapable of returning. The organization of events, the situation that *is* the story, as read by Borges, is more important than the man Wakefield, an insignificant, disposable character, a "nincompoop" in Hawthorne's words. Like Max Beerbohm's Enoch Soames, Wakefield is the ideally empty, somewhat obtuse character, embodying a narrative situation in order to exist. Yet in his telling of the story, Borges significantly alters Hawthorne's Wakefield; tempted by the author's rhetorical question—"What kind of a man is Wakefield? . . . We have complete freedom to shape out the idea we have of him and give him the name of Wakefield"[3]—he reshapes the character. Paring down Hawthorne's loquacious, heavily didactic "shaping out" of Wakefield, Borges reduces the character to a sentence but then adds other details that do not appear in the story. In a word, he reshapes Wakefield as he reads him:

> [A] calm man, timidly vain, selfish, given to childish mysteries and the keeping of insignificant secrets; a dispassionate man of great imaginative and mental prowess, but capable of long, idle, leisurely, inconclusive, and vague meditations. (OI 54)

This compact description faithfully corresponds to the facts given by Hawthorne's story but for one detail. Hawthorne conclusively states that "Imagination, in the proper meaning of the term, made no part of Wakefield's gifts" (158). In his reshaping of Wakefield, Borges ignores this impoverishing limitation: Hawthorne's "nincompoop" is sympathetically transformed into a man of "great imaginative and mental prowess."

There is more. Hawthorne's text explicitly points to a gesture made by the character. Leaving his home for the first time, Wakefield closes the door behind him, then opens it a bit and smiles. His wife does not forget that smile, which would feed her fantasies during twenty long, lonely years. And then, when Wakefield finally returns home, before closing the door, he smiles again: "The crafty smile we already know is hovering, ghostlike, on his face. At last Wakefield has returned" (OI 56). The original story and its succinct retelling by Borges coincide up to this point. In both, the same smile opens and closes the journey of a man who, according to Hawthorne, "by stepping aside for a moment . . . exposes himself to a fearful risk of losing his place forever" (169). But Borges does more than just retain that double smile: he expands it. His Wakefield smiles when Hawthorne's does not; when the man, assured of the distance he has created by his departure, reaches the shelter he has prepared for himself not far from home: "He makes himself comfortable by the fireplace and smiles" (OI 54). In that isolated refuge, the emblematic smile that frames Wakefield's adventure becomes a more mysterious, individual gesture: highlighted for an instant, in Borges's rendering of the story, it makes the actor more visible than the situation.

The web of theories presented by Borges in "Nathaniel Hawthorne" to justify his reading is carefully detailed. It is also carefully insidious. One should recall that one of the aims of this essay is to show that Hawthorne's short stories are superior to his novels because in the stories narrative situation takes precedent over character. Yet paradoxically, in his reading of this *story*, Borges draws attention less to situation than to character. Similarly, nine years before his essay on Hawthorne, in his prologue to Bioy Casares's *The Invention of Morel*, again paradoxically, speaking of a *novel* (which according to him should exhibit the dominance of character over situation), Borges praises the superiority of plot over individuals.[4] He admiringly compares Bioy Casares's novel to Kafka's *The Trial* and to James's *The Turn of the Screw*, texts that certainly do not copy reality's "teeming ways," as Borges says with disdain, nor do they invite the reader to share vicariously in the life of a character. Thus, the boundaries between genres become arbitrary, as does the importance of the elements, character, or narrative situation, which supposedly define those genres. And yet it is Borges himself who has proposed such questionable boundaries from the beginning. It is no wonder that the name of Benedetto Croce, classifier and destabilizer of literary genres, appears rather frequently in the work of Borges. What Borges says of Croce's arguments might be said of Borges's own comments on the short story and the novel, on plot and character: they "serve to cut short a discussion, not to resolve it" (R 30).

Borges's "web of theories" on fiction is unpredictable, contradictory, permanently shifting. The terms of his argument are less important than their blurring, less important than the reciprocal contamination to which he subjects them. Far from setting up rigid categories, his statements create doubt, hesitation; they work against fixed definitions. The theoretical swerves in the essay on Hawthorne, in the prologue to the novel by Bioy Casares, and in both texts when read jointly, are but a few examples of the shifting dynamics of every Borges text. Reassuring binarisms are systematically disrupted, fractured by the possibility of a rift, a fault that disturbs all certainties and finally undoes them. That "fault," so often read as a deficiency by critics eager for clear-cut boundaries, marks from the beginning Borges's process of composition. The text is written and read with no securities, on the edge, where language is articulated and shattered at the same time.

"The Coveter of Souls":
A First Step toward Fiction

The shifting dynamics characteristic of Borges are thematically suggested in his early poetry. *Fervor de Buenos Aires, Luna de enfrente,* and *Cuaderno San Martín* renew in an odd way the fluctuating perspective of the Benjaminian *flâneur,* the gaze of an idle stroller in the twilight of a city that is no longer his, or rather that is only his at twilight. It is a city that he *discovers* alone, grasping the bits and pieces that escaped him during the day and claiming them for his own in a solitary ritual. *Flâneur-voyeur:* yet physical displacement is not a condition necessary to attentive idleness nor to vicarious voraciousness. Borges's *flâneur,* isolated in his modest walks through the outskirts of Buenos Aires, resorts, from his very first essays, to literary strolls, to textual *voyeurism.* He admires William Hudson's *The Purple Land* as:

> [T]he book of a coveter of lives, of someone who takes pleasure in the variants of the "I." Hudson never loses his temper with his readers, never taunts them or scolds them, never doubts this democratic truth: that the other is also an "I," and that for him I am an "other" or perhaps a "would-that-he-not-be." Hudson proposes, and justifies, that each soul he examines is unique, that its virtues, its flaws, even the peculiarities of its mistakes, are irreplaceable. In this way he traces memorable destinies. . . . Those lives, and the ones in the series of stories called *The Ombú,* are not eternal archetypes; they are episodic and real, like the ones invented by God. To witness them is to take on new lives— luminous, often noble—and to broaden the "I" into a multitude. (TE 35)

Borges's voyeurism, in spite of its apparently expansive enthusiasm ("to broaden the 'I' into a multitude"), introduces a doubt affecting not only "the variants of the 'I'" but the "I" itself reading the text: "the other is also an 'I,' and . . . for him I am an 'other' or perhaps a 'would-that-he-not-be'." In any event, the doubt cast over being—being self, being other, not being at all—de-centers. It is from this ontological hesitation, this "would-that-it-not-be," that one must look at Borges's fiction. In his 1925 essay, "La nadería de la personalidad" [The Nothingness of Personality], Borges had already written: "I aim to prove that personality is a chimera sustained by habit and conceit, with neither metaphysical support nor intrinsic reality. Therefore, I want to subject literature to the consequences flowing from those premises. On those premises, I wish to elaborate an aesthetic principle that will oppose the psychologism left to us by the last century" (I 84).

"There is no such thing as an 'I' capable of sustaining its unity," adds Borges. Taking the text a small step further, one could add that there is no sustained *unity*. In this early essay, Borges merely registers doubt. The subject of narration (one may temporarily call it 'character' since it arises from a reflection on personality), is as elusive as the fragmented, slippery "I."

Greedy Sequels:
Evaristo Carriego and the "Infamous Biographies"

That one person should wish to arouse in another memories relating only to a third person is an obvious paradox. To pursue this paradox freely is the harmless intention of all biographies. The fact of my having known Carriego does not, I contend—not in this particular case—modify the difficulty of this undertaking. I have in my possession memories of Carriego: memories of memories of other memories, whose slightest distortions, at the very outset, may have increased imperceptibly at each retelling. These memories preserve, I am sure, the particular flavor that I call Carriego and that allows us to pick out one face in a crowd. Be that as it may, such a store of inconsequential memories—his tone of voice, the way he walked, the way he idled, the expression in his eyes—is that part of my information about him which least lends itself to the pen. (EC 51)

The harmless intention of all biographies: how would *Evaristo Carriego*, a book "which is less documentary than imaginative" (EC 34), fit within the genre? Presented as an attempt to capture an "unforgettable destiny" the book is anything but that. The harmless biography turns out to be a wily, edgy text. The second chapter, which might have been considered central, "A Life of Evaristo Carriego," presents only a shadowy outline of a character, deliberately chosen for his provincial quality, his modesty; indeed, when other voices advised Borges to write about a more central poet—

say, Lugones—Borges persisted in his election of a second-rate bard.[5] Borges's narrative theories notwithstanding, there are very few enduring traits, like Wakefield's smile, which would make Carriego "come alive." The narrator's "disjointed work . . . should be to make . . . information visual" (EC 55); yet "A Life of Evaristo Carriego" boils down more to reports about the man than to visual images of him.

The error lies in assuming that "A Life of Evaristo Carriego" is necessarily the central chapter, the real biographical core of a text that should make unequivocal sense of someone's life. In a later essay, "About William Beckford's *Vathek*," Borges recalls the witticism attributed by Wilde to Carlyle, the project of writing "a biography of Michelangelo that would omit any mention of Michelangelo's works." And Borges adds:

> Reality is so complex, history is so fragmented and so simplified, that an omniscient observer could write an indefinite, and almost infinite, number of biographies of a man, each of which would emphasize different facts; we would have to read many of them before we realized that the protagonist was the same man. . . . A history of a man's dreams is not inconceivable; or of the organs of his body; or of the mistakes he has made; or of all the moments when he imagined the Pyramids; or of his traffic with night and with dawn. (OI 137)

From the very title of the second chapter, "A Life of Evaristo Carriego," Borges's text suggests that *one* of many possible stories has been chosen. The narrator's "disjointed work" is more engaged in the detailed re-creation of a man's environment, his periphery, so to speak, than in the actual recounting of personal anecdote: "friends, like the dead, and like cities, help make up a man" (EC 60). The make-up of the character called "Carriego" certainly relies on a montage of images, but they are indirect images of Carriego—images of sections of Buenos Aires called Palermo, Maldonado, Tierra del Fuego—that "acknowledge and allude to him" (EC 64). "A man, after all, amounts to his circumstances" (A 119), writes Borges in a subsequent fiction. In the same way, for his biographer, Carriego "knew himself to be frail and mortal, but the endless pink-walled streets of Palermo kept him going" (EC 57).

It is no accident that the preface to this early text by Borges celebrates the rejection of enclosure, of a double enclosure: "I grew up in a garden, behind a fence of iron palings, and in a library of endless English books" (EC 33). To narrate, in *Evaristo Carriego*, is to overstep boundaries. In the same way that the Borges *flâneur* displaced the center of the city toward its periphery, the narrator of *Evaristo Carriego* displaces familiar patterns of biographical narration toward the margins, in order to find out "what was going on, meanwhile, on the other side of the iron palings" (EC 33).

This double perspective—the closure of a fixed "inside"; the mobility of an "outside" that questions the closure—sets off, in *Evaristo Carriego*, the fluctuation that frames Borges's fiction. The ambiguity of the essays in *Inquisiciones* [Inquisitions] and *El tamaño de mi esperanza* [The Breadth of My Hope] persists in this text. The "coveter of souls" is thankful for the "rustle of lives" offered by a Buenos Aires that he conjures both for Carriego and for himself; a rustle of lives at once familiar and distant, like those unique destinies described by Hudson or perceived by the *flâneur*. Honduras street, Borges writes, referring to an incident in Carriego's life, "felt it had acquired more substance when it saw itself in print" (EC 62). No doubt the narrator in *Evaristo Carriego* also feels more substantial when he finds "unexpected solace" in repeating the imaginary gestures of another: drinking a large glass of country wine, plucking a sprig of honeysuckle as he walks by a wall (EC 63). The gestures conjured by the story give life to the storyteller. The narrator of *Evaristo Carriego* makes a pact with a mediocre poet, Carriego, in order to write himself into a biography that serves him as a pre-text.

Nevertheless, the Borges of "La nadería de la personalidad" curtails, in *Evaristo Carriego*, the effects of the rustle of lives and is wary of his sympathy for individual destinies. He insists on fragmenting Carriego as a character, presenting him (and presenting himself) *en abîme*, defined by his very displacement: "a mode of truth, not of truth coherent and central, but angular and splintered," reads the epigraph from De Quincey that questions the very unity of the self. If there are references in *Evaristo Carriego* to "identity," this identity must be *plural, fleeting, disperse*: "as if Carriego went on living in our lives, as if for a few seconds each one of us were Carriego" (EC 63). The text of *Evaristo Carriego* is a place of convergence and divergence. Like Pierre Menard's *Quixote*, it is a contingent place where the biographer, the future maker of fictions, undertakes the possibility of re-creating and inscribing a character, but it is also a place where he inaugurates the possibility of erasing the very character he has inscribed.

"A Surface of Images"

If *Evaristo Carriego* is an attempt to record what lies "on the other side of the iron palings" (EC 33) by a first person precariously juggling inside and outside, *A Universal History of Infamy* celebrates the crossing of a boundary. Its textual approach retains certain techniques from *Evaristo Carriego*: a montage characterized by isolated traits, the supposedly visual bent of the text, the fragmented character, the deferred denouement. Yet the sympathy of the narrator for his narrative subject, emphasized in *Evaristo Carriego* through the use of the first person, disappears: the coveter of souls becomes a coveter of stories. The outside to which the stories in *A Universal History of Infamy* seem to refer is neither beyond the iron palings nor on this side of them. The "infamous biographies" do away with topographical illusion; the impulse behind fiction now points to a purely literary space. *A Universal History of Infamy* is "the irresponsible game of a shy young man who dared not write stories and so amused himself by falsifying and distorting (without any aesthetic justification whatever) the tales of others" (UHI 11–12).

Such a statement clearly marks the distance covered. In *Evaristo Carriego*, the narrator simultaneously shatters the character and identifies with him, fleetingly, through images that shape both the story and the narrator himself. In *A Universal History of Infamy* the narrator does not take possession of biography, does not account for the life of another so as to account for himself; rather, he takes possession of the other's *stories*. The difference between the two approaches is tenuous if we consider the narrative pre-texts that are put to use: there would seem to be no basic difference between Borges reading the life of Evaristo Carriego and his reading the life of the improbable impostor Tom Castro. However, the narrator must readjust his greed: he no longer covets a no-man's land like Carriego's Palermo, which he invents as he goes along, but rather ventures into an apparently closed unit, a text written by another. Cannibalism now becomes conversation.

Conspicuously missing from the "infamous biographies" presented by Borges is the nostalgic voice, "languid with love," which spoke to us of Carriego. On the contrary, Borges insists on highlighting the artifice of his narrative scheme. The stories in *A Universal History of Infamy*, he writes in the preface, blatantly resort to "random enumerations, sudden shifts of continuity, and the paring down of a man's whole life to two or three scenes . . . . They are not, they do not try to be, psychological" (UHI 13). The preface is generous in its recognition of sources. Two of them, Stevenson and von Sternberg, are significant, precisely because of their attempts to define fiction as artifice allowing for recognition but not identification, however fleeting that identification might be.[6]

A Universal History of Infamy does not count on sympathy to bond narrator, reader, and characters or settings. On the contrary, Borges curbs all pathos; the very title of the book, in its excess, flaunts the deliberately parodic intent of Borges's reading: "Scaffolds and pirates populate it, and the word 'infamy' in the title is thunderous, but behind the sound and fury there is nothing. The book is no more than appearance, than a surface of images; for that very reason, it may prove enjoyable" (UHI 12).[7] The exaggeration and parodic intent of *A Universal History of Infamy* block the fragmentary identification posited in *Evaristo Carriego*. There is no extratextual reality (as in the case of Carriego's Palermo) to share. There is no "original" text to recognize since it is, in fact, fragmented, pieced together again, and above all, *remote*. Exaggeration (based on a reading of texts, not of lives) thwarts any possible recognition, or rather veers away from it. *A Universal History of Infamy* turns to previous stories in order to tell them differently; the narrating subject, deliberately eclipsed as a *person*, blocks the passage toward a compassionate "we." While the only thing left is a "surface of images," barely an appearance, defying interpretation, it sets off a multiplicity of dialogues and of possible, variously interchangeable complicities. There is dialogue and connivance between a narrating subject, devoid of all personal markings, and a borrowed story which he tells and which tells on him, as narrator; there is dialogue between a text and its pre-text, initiating a textual exchange; there is dialogue, finally between a reader and an author who come into contact through the duplicity of parody, a contact based either on a shared referent, or on the conventionally hyperbolic remoteness proposed by the stories.

If the presentation of character in *A Universal History of Infamy* is, as in *Evaristo Carriego*, indirect and metonymic, the aim is different: not to familiarize but to puzzle the reader, to move him or her to another level. Borges's previous comments on the tenuousness of personality—the "I," the "other," the "would-that-he-not-be"—that give an unsettling spark to his notion of character, lead, in the protofictions of *A Universal History of Infamy*, to the abolition of personal traits. Compare, for example, the deliberately conversational, understated tone of the first chapter in *Evaristo Carriego*, "Palermo, Buenos Aires," to the barrage of images and the intentional irony in the first pages of "The Dread Redeemer Lazarus Morell" or of "Monk Eastman, Purveyor of Iniquities." In these two texts the reader also approaches the main character indirectly. "The Dread Redeemer" is divided into almost didactic metonymic sequences: from "The Remote Cause" of slavery to "The Place" where it takes hold, from the place to "The Men" who inhabit it, from the men to "The Man." From the man, the shift is to a detailed description of the action, faithfully following the metonymic sequence through contiguity and mocking it at the same time: "The Method," "Final Release," "The Cataclysm."

Significantly, the cataclysm does not end in denouement, but in "The Disruption." This nonending of a carefully disrupted fiction, thwarting all hope of "poetic justice (or poetic symmetry)" (UHI 28), only echoes the process of delay and interruption at work in "The Dread Redeemer" from the very beginning, a process undermining the causal linearity that the headings of the different sections would appear to suggest. The oxymoronic excess of the story's title is at work in each one of those sections. Like proliferating scenes in a Baroque engraving, these sections question and obstruct, in their very excess, the simplest narrative sequence. Take for example, in the section of the story subtitled "The Remote Cause," the hyperbolic consequences attributed to the missionary zeal of Bartolomé de Las Casas, traditionally, and not entirely justifiably, held responsible for the introduction of slavery in the New World:

> In 1517, the Spanish missionary Bartolomé de las Casas, taking great pity on the Indians who were languishing in the hellish workpits of Antillean gold mines, suggested to Charles V, king of Spain, a scheme for importing blacks, so that they might languish in the hellish workpits of Antillean gold mines. To this odd philanthropic twist we owe, all up and down the America,

endless things—W. C. Handy's blues; the Parisian success of the Uruguayan lawyer and painter of Negro genre, Don Pedro Figari; the solid native prose of another Uruguayan, don Vicente Rossi, who traced the origin of the tango to Negroes; the mythological dimensions of Abraham Lincoln; the five hundred thousand dead of the Civil War and its three thousand three hundred millions spent in military pensions; the entrance of the verb "to lynch" in the thirteenth edition of the dictionary of the Spanish Academy; King Vidor's impetuous film *Hallelujah*; the lusty bayonet charge led by the Argentine captain Miguel Soler, at the head of his famous regiment of "Mulattoes and Blacks," in the Uruguayan battle of Cerrito; the vivacious charm of Miss So and So; the Negro killed by Martín Fierro; the deplorable Cuban rumba "The Peanut Vendor"; the arrested, dungeon-ridden Napoleonism of Toussaint L'Ouverture; the cross and the snake of Haitian voodoo rites and the blood of goats whose throats were slit by the *papaloi's* machete; the *habanera*, mother of the tango; another old Negro dance, of Buenos Aires and Montevideo, the *candombe*. (UHI 19–20)

Given the genealogical pretension of its title, "The Remote Cause," this catalog seems on the one hand to demand that the reader focus on every detail: yet on the other, its festive nature, calling attention only to itself, obstructs such a proleptic reading. In a blatant process of bricolage, the catalog brings together recognizable historical fact, household mythology, literary allusion, arbitrary personal opinion, private joke, and slander. It is a series that levels the elements that constitute it, as will, later on, in other texts by Borges, the no less uneven erudite enumerations. Interrupting a story that has barely begun, it tempts the reader with two alternatives, two ways of pacing the reading, difficult to reconcile with each other. On the one hand, the reader is lured by the urgency of successive discoveries, as promised in the title of the story's first section, "The Remote Cause," and apparently confirmed by the subsequent section headings. A reader thus prompted will not stop, for example, at the biased local complicity suggested by "the vivacious charm of Miss So and So." On the other hand, the reader is tempted by the exact opposite, by the sustained pleasure of a paragraph whose accumulation of detail cancels all possible anticipation and proposes, with each new element in the series, the possibility of deviating from the continuity of the story. It should be noted that the two possibilities and the two reading times work simultaneously in the first part of "The Dread Redeemer Lazarus Morell." The series ends up after all with the presentation of the character on whom the biography is supposedly centered, as another entry in the series or as an afterthought: "And, further, the great and blameworthy life of the nefarious redeemer Lazarus Morell" (UHI 20). The uneven enumeration that precedes him taints this nefarious redeemer. The chaotic series of the first paragraph does not allow the character a centrality; rather it displaces him. Thus unhinged, his carnivalesque nature becomes all the more apparent.

Games with Masks

Silvina Ocampo writes that Borges is upset by masks and disguises.[8] However, when Richard Burgin asks him during one of his interviews what he thinks of the theater, the first play that comes to Borges's mind is O'Neill's *The Great God Brown*, literally a masquerade (Burgin 108). And when Burgin asks about *A Universal History of Infamy*, Borges answers, "All the stories in that volume were mockeries in some way, artifices" (Burgin 28). What else indeed is that "appearance," that "surface of images," if not a mockery of other texts and a textual carnival?

Let me return to the "infamous biographies" and to the hyperbolic characters supposedly centering them. In these texts that claim to be primarily visual, physical descriptions are rare; characters are never submitted to "the enumeration and definition of the parts of a whole"[9] with the illusion of endowing them with a unique, intelligible, or memorable face. In an essay recalling the presentation of characters in Gabriel Miró, Borges concludes rather smugly: "Thirteen or fourteen elements make up the chaotic series; the author invites us to conceive those *disjecta membra* and coordinate them in a single, coherent image. Such a mental operation is impracticable: no one is able to imagine type X feet, add to them a type Y throat, and then type Z cheeks. . . ."

The operation is indeed impracticable if one attempts to *visualize* a character who, even with fewer than the thirteen or fourteen elements with which Miró describes Herodias, is after all a verbal construct. Borges denounces the "fallacy of the visual that rules in literature" (IA 84). "I write *images*," he states, "fully aware of the treachery of that word" (IA 83). However, in the same essay, given the choice between that treacherous term and the term *intuition*, proposed instead by Croce, Borges prefers *image*:

> I write *images*, a word as treacherous as the other, but I write about treacheries that count and that the history of literature (or rather, the self-styled history of a self-styled literature) should not pass over, since most of its material comes from those very treacheries. It is a common error to suppose that the images communicated by a writer should be preferably visual. Such an error has its etymological justification: *imago* means simulacrum, apparition, effigy, form, sometimes sheath (which mimics the steel blade waiting to enter it), also echo, *vocalis imago*, and the conception of a thing. Thus says the biography of that word and that biography is misleading. (IA 84)

Imago, effigy, apparition: the words stress the treacherous nature of the simulacrum. Significantly, Borges's criticism of Miró would lose some of its negative charge if it did not refer to the simulacrum of a *person*. Applied to a *text*, Borges's comment would not be unsound: "The author invites us to conceive those *disjecta membra* and coordinate them in a single, coherent image." More than a mere criticism of Miró's literary technique, the statement might characterize Borges's own text, although, were the statement applied to him, Borges might qualify the final words: a single, coherent image that is always in the process of undoing itself. The *disjecta membra* of Miró's characters are as difficult to coordinate as the heterogeneous elements in the first paragraph of "The Dread Redeemer Lazarus Morell." They stop the reader, thwarting him in his efforts to bring cohesion to the disparate.

A difference in rhetoric no doubt distances Borges from Miró yet it does not wholly account for his critique. What seems to provoke Borges is the fact that Miró's *disjecta membra* are coordinated into an anthropomorphic image: a character, not a text. And when in a later book, *Historia de la eternidad* [A History of Eternity], Borges praises the enumeration of *disjecta membra* to signify a personified whole, he conspicuously chooses an example clearly rendered *impersonal* by the use of rhetorical devices. More than a descriptive enumeration, the one he cites is a ritualistic one, in which *topoi* construct an icon and protect it from the threat of novel elements:

> To hear the description of a queen—hair like nights of flight and exile but a face like a dawn of delights, breasts like ivory spheres lending their light to the moons, a walk that would shame the antelopes and make the willows rage, hips so ample that she cannot stand, feet as narrow as the tip of a spear—and to fall in love with her unto pleasure and unto death, is one of the traditional themes of the *Thousand and One Nights*. (HE 22)

The description of that inconceivable whole—impossible to visualize as an image—clearly differs from an anthropomorphic simulacrum. The image functions on another level. The queen's *disjecta membra* are fused by the "generic" traits that unite them: the generic "takes precedence over individual traits, *which are tolerated thanks to that precedence*" (HE 22). The text cancels the individual it describes, an individual impossible to represent in a single image. It translates the character into all too familiar, conventional signs, denying it any original traits, masking it, quite literally, with writing.

Thus, even though disguises may bother Borges the man, the characters in *A Universal History of Infamy*, while portrayed through isolated traits or circumstantial detail, finally only gain coherence through disguise. The *disjecta membra* that should have come together into a single image do not; their dispersion is concealed, instead, by a mask. The *figuration* of a character (so laboriously synecdochic in Miró) becomes an openly metaphoric simulacrum in *A Universal History of Infamy*.

More than on infamy—a colorful sin—these stories are founded on another sort of transgression: the fear of using words (and the ensuing temptation to use words) to create personal images, images capable of referring, even in a fragmentary way, to a referent that could be more than mere circumstance, that could be an actual individual. For the first time Borges fully comes to grips with the composition of a fictional character, a character not sustained by personal nostalgia, or by memories of others, but by disconnected words. He ventures to create such a character while showing the inadequacy or the flaw of his creation, a mere effigy.

The infamous masks of *A Universal History of Infamy* mark an important turning point in Borges's reflection on fiction. It is worthy of note that, in order to begin writing fiction, Borges resorts not just to "worn out," borrowed material, as in *Evaristo Carriego*, but to material that, in addition, carries the stigma of infamy. In this climate of duplicity and betrayal, Borges's earlier theoretical reflections are both applied and contradicted, thus inaugurating, on the level of narration, a critical dialogue that will gain depth in later fictions and essays. Mask and face confront each other, in a challenging, fertile counterpoint.

Mask and Displacement

We know everything about Lazarus Morell—everything the story gives us—except what the story will not give: a central image of the character. The absence of a face is compounded by the abundance of false visages: "The daguerreotypes of Morell usually published in American magazines are not authentic. This lack of genuine representation of so memorable and famous a man cannot be accidental. We may suppose that Morell resisted the camera, essentially, so as not to leave behind pointless clues, and, at the same time, to foster the mystery that surrounded him" (UHI 22). The features listed in the narrator's description of Morell hardly establish a unique personal image. The emphasis is on cliché, endowed with emblematic proportions. Perhaps Lazarus Morell's most outstanding trait is that he dies, as it were, against the grain. Deviating from the conventionally daring conduct attributed to him in the story, he dies a different, less sensational death: not hanged, not drowned, but in a hospital bed. The heroic cliché sustaining his previous actions is suddenly abandoned: the final section, subtitled "The Disruption," breaks with the story of the lucky, unpunished outlaw and returns to the nothingness of his personality: the man who refused to have his photograph taken chooses to die under a false name. The story should be read as a repertory of foreseeable exploits, framed by two masks: the false daguerreotype at the beginning and the final pseudonym that ends, or rather interrupts, the narrative.

Deception, lack of "genuine effigies," false names, are the basic resources of *A Universal History of Infamy*. There is no place—that is, there is no center—for these personified simulacra that function as shifters throughout the stories. "Tom Castro, the Implausible Impostor" is a vacancy, alternately occupied and emptied. One Arthur Orton, longing for a break ("Running away to sea is, for the English, the traditional break from paternal authority" [UHI 31]), becomes Tom Castro, who becomes Roger Charles Tichborne, who becomes nothing. The situation that might be deemed central here—the imposture of the Tichborne claimant—is undermined inside and out. As in the case of Lazarus Morell, the story is framed by a twofold divergence from the name of origin: an alias at the beginning (Tom Castro), anonymity at the end. Moreover, Tichborne, the object of imposture, the dead man whose place Orton/Castro takes, is in himself an estranged character, full of unusual attributes emphasizing his difference: he was an *English* nobleman, he belonged to a *Catholic* family, and spoke English with the most refined *Parisian* accent. For that reason, the text adds, he awoke in others (as difference inevitably does) "incomparable resentment" (UHI 34). One could hardly imagine a more imposing, inaccessible mask for Arthur Orton, son of Wapping butchers, but for the fact that the original on whom the mask would be fashioned was already marked by divergence; was already, himself, something of a mask.

A mask for Roger Tichborne, Orton/Castro is also the mask of dead Ebenezer Bogle, the schemer behind the imposture: "Tom Castro was the ghost of Roger Charles Tichborne, but he was a sorry ghost animated by someone else's genius" (UHI 37). Like Lazarus Morell, he ends his days without an identity, contradicting himself. He would give "little lectures in which he alternately pleaded his innocence or his guilt. Modesty and ingratiation were so deep-seated in him that many a night he would begin by exoneration and end by confession, always disposed to the leanings of his audience" (UHI 38). His confusions and contradictions bring to mind the Homer of "The Immortal": "it is famous that after singing of the war in Ilion, he sang of the war of the frogs and the mice" (L 114).

Masks, aliases, props, theatrical settings are the very substance of these stories. The hollow protagonist of "Monk Eastman, Purveyor of Iniquities," is called Edward Ostermann, alias Edward Delaney, alias William Delaney, alias Joseph Marvin, alias Joseph Morris, alias Monk Eastman. In "The Disinterested Killer Bill Harrigan," a freckled Irish boy, brought up among blacks, goes from playing the "slum rat" to playing Billy the Kid, the flamboyant outlaw of the Wild West. Theatricality touches him even after his death: "He was shaved, sheathed in ready-made clothes, and displayed to awe and ridicule in the window of Fort Sumner's biggest store. Men on horseback and in buckboards gathered for miles and miles around. On the third day, they had to use make-up on him. On the fourth day, he was buried with rejoicing" (UHI 66).

Theatricality and imposture, both ritualized, are essential to "The Insulting Master of Etiquette, Kotsuké no Suké." In this story, there is an envoy who *represents* the Mikado; there is a master of *ceremonies* instructing the master of the Tower of Akô on how to act before the envoy. Death itself—as punishment for a breach of ritual—becomes a spectacle: the master of Akô ritually commits suicide before an audience, on a carefully prepared stage, and "because of the red felt the more distant spectators were unable to see blood" (UHI 71). In order to avenge his retainer, Kuranosuké feigns to be the man that he is not and it is the imposture that brings him victory.

The Mask Revealed

Borges's "infamous biographies" culminate, almost didactically, in the carnivalesque baroque of "The Masked Dyer, Hakim of Merv," a story in which everything, including the individual's original face, is a mask. Borges mentions this story, among others, in the prologue to *Evaristo Carriego*. In the childhood home behind the fence of iron palings, Khurasan's veiled prophet was one of the characters who "populated my days and gave a pleasurable shiver to my nights" (EC 33). In *A Universal History of Infamy*, Borges adds a correction; he calls him "the Veiled Prophet, or more accurately, the *Masked* Prophet of Khurasan" (UHI 79; my emphasis).

As Roger Caillois has noted, the historical sources that Borges resorts to are themselves masked in his tale.[10] Ignoring them, the story also strays, as might be expected, from the accounts unanimously recorded in those established, reliable chronicles for which it has little use. None of those chronicles, for example, mentions the prophet's leprosy, nor his final unmasking. Also masked—that is, blurred by anonymity, oblivion, or artifice—are the elements that might give texture to the character. In the same way that

Borges will later engage in false attributions and apocrypha, he now attributes an inaccessible canonical book to the prophet. *The Annihilation of the Rose* is supposedly a rebuttal of an earlier, possibly apocryphal, heretical text: the *Dark Rose*, or *Hidden Rose*, which "is lost, for the manuscript found in 1899 and published all too hastily by the *Morgenländisches Archiv* has been pronounced a forgery" (UHI 79). As an additional, blurry reminder of the man who was Hakim of Merv, there remain a few coins whose effigies have been erased.

In Borges's version, the life of the prophet is a sustained practice of dissimulation. It is known that as a youth he was skilled in the trade of dyer, "that craft of the ungodly, the counterfeiter, and the shifty, that was to inspire him to the first imprecations of his unbridled career": "Thus did I sin in the days of my youth, tampering with the true colors of God's creation. The Angel told me that the ram was not the color of the tiger, the Satan told me that the Almighty wanted them to be, and that He was availing himself of my skill and my dyestuffs. Now I know that the Angel and the Satan both strayed from the truth, and that all colors are abominable" (UHI 80).

Borges's story is an exercise in theatrical distancing, where everything is something else and everything lacks its orginal effigy (or name). Like Tom Castro, encouraged by Bogle, the deceitful dyer is skillful in choosing the mask that best contradicts him. He chooses a brutal bull's mask to contradict his singularly sweet voice; a fourfold white veil, "the most contradictory," in order to conquer a province whose emblematic color is black (UHI 83). Hakim's God is a "spectral god . . . as majestically devoid of origin as of name and face" (UHI 84). For Hakim the world itself is a masquerade: "a mistake, a clumsy parody. Mirrors and fatherhood, because they multiply and confirm that world, are abominations" (UHI 84). Finally the leper prophet's real face, the hidden face his disillusioned followers discover, functions as a disguise: "It was so bloated and unbelievable that to the mass of onlookers it seemed a mask" (UHI 86).

Instead of functioning as points of convergence, the characters in *A Universal History of Infamy* are effective points of divergence. They are and are not their masks; rather, they fleetingly occupy those masks, without revealing themselves. Incidentally, the chosen masks are usually masks that have been previously *read*: the character often recognizes in a text (or in a spectacle) the face or the name he will use as a mask. Tom Castro/Arthur Orton becomes himself as he reads Tichborne's diary. During his New York apprenticeship, Billy the Kid enjoyed seeing cowboy melodramas in the Bowery playhouses. The rebellious widow Ching's final recognition, in a show of masks put on by the emperor's forces, leads her to change her sign and take on a new persona. The act of reading gels, and at the same time deflects, identity.

Based on borrowed stories, alienated within his own story, the character sketched by Borges in *A Universal History of Infamy* is an elusive conglomerate. Fragmented, robbed of centrality by the importance given to his circumstance, at once vacant and shielded by masks, Borges's character is, like Orson Welles's *Citizen Kane*, "a simulacrum, a chaos of appearances,"[11] a surface of images whose stability is permanently threatened by multiplicity and hiatus. Borges masks and unmasks character, his use of character, as he will later mask and unmask other rhetorical devices, other narrative props.

When speaking of *A Universal History of Infamy*, Borges states that "it amused me when I wrote it, but I can hardly recall who the characters were" (Burgin 28). Little remains indeed of these unmemorable masks but for some isolated feature, contributing less to the visual intent proclaimed in the text than to an action that it supports directly or in counterpoint. The description of Tom Castro is necessary in order to celebrate his imposture (Roger Tichborne is his physical opposite), in order to prove "the virtues of disparity" (UHI 33). The description of Monk Eastman is also established *against* something. Against the "pudgy, epicene Capone" (UHI 54), to begin with, but above all to affirm the contrast between frailness and brute force that holds up the story. Eastman, with his "short, bull neck; a barrel chest; long, scrappy arms . . . and legs bowed out like a cowboy's or a sailor's" (UHI 54), makes the rounds of his territory with a dove on his shoulder, "just like a bull with a cowbird on its rump" (UHI 54). Only rarely do the texts of *A Universal History of Infamy* indulge in purely gratuitous traits: a shining bald pate that Billy the Kid finds irresistible, the bare feet of Lazarus Morell pacing darkened rooms. Loose traits appear frequently, as a resource, in Borges's later texts; they allow for the pleasure, not of description (which Borges finds tedious), but of unaccountable detail.

2

Textual Rubrications

Let us say briefly that the book can always be signed, it remains indifferent to who signs it; the work—Festivity as disaster—requires resignation, requires that whoever claims to write it renounce himself and cease to designate himself.

Then why do we sign our books? Out of modesty, as a way of saying: these are still only books, indifferent to signatures.

Maurice Blanchot, "The Absence of the Book"

It is precisely because I forget that I read.

Roland Barthes, *S/Z*

The Signs in a Book

"That one person should wish to arouse in another memories relating only to a third person is an obvious paradox" (EC 51). Referred to fiction, the statement remains as provocative as it is when applied to biography. Borges's fiction trips the simple scheme *sender-message-receiver*, delaying and complicating each one of its stages, erasing distinctions, simultaneously multiplying the narrative possibilities of dialogue. The author addresses the reader and at the same time presents himself as a reader, a receiver of his own message: "between our 'naughts' there is little difference; the fact that you are the reader of these exercises and I its writer is trivial and fortuitous" (OP 15). The devices that make this perpetually reversible dialogue are, at the same time, a vehicle for communication and its obstacle. In Borges's text, the written letter cuts into the dialogue, interpolates its own space and demands its own voice, disturbing the already precarious exchange between sender and receiver, between author-reader and reader-author: as if that which is spoken, that which does not actively participate in the dialogue, were suddenly tainted by the "persons" who allude to it in their exchange. The same contamination that blurs the limits between sender and receiver, between author and reader, also bears on the text, unlimiting it. Turned into an active, though sometimes uneasy participant, the text inflects all parties involved in its articulation, in the same way that it inflects pre-texts and subsequent texts referring to it. Borges takes pleasure in expanding and recharging a narrative message that is far from being fixed and inert: a message that enfolds those who write it, narrate it, read it, and at the same time, a message that is dispersed among them all. There is little difference between writer and reader, as there is little difference between writer and text, between text and reader, between the "visible" text and its pre-text: they are interchangeable participants, on equal footing.

"Pierre Menard, Author of the *Quixote*" is Borges's first fiction. It is not, of course, his first fictional work: *Evaristo Carriego*, *A Universal History of Infamy*, and "The Approach to al-Mu'tasim" have already been written, but "Pierre Menard" is the first fiction acknowledged by Borges as such. He singles it out as a deliberate break: "Then I decided to write something, but something new and different for me, so that, if it failed, I could blame it on the novelty of the effort."[1] Borges considered that the stories he had written before were not really stories; they were commentaries of other books or mock bibliographical notes.

This much touted rupture is less convincing than it would appear, less innovative than what Borges's disingenuous statement would lead one to believe. On the contrary, rather than a break, "Pierre Menard" distinctly marks the continuity between itself and the fiction preceding it, whether or not Borges called them stories. If there is a change, it resides not in the choice of a new genre but in the advertisement of processes that operated on the sly in his previous texts. "Pierre Menard" does not launch Borges's fiction; it simply confirms it.

If one looks for conventional narrative elements in this first "story" by Borges, one will be more than disappointed, just as one was duped by Evaristo Carriego's "biography," which clearly mocked the rules of the game. In "Pierre Menard" nothing *happens*. This should not necessarily be construed as a drawback; nothing

much happens in James's fiction, after all, as the author himself
points out. However, while James's narrative substitutes direct action with complex psychological texture—in James, psychological
tension *is* action—Borges's narrative does away with action, character, and psychology. The complex "adventure" that ultimately
constitutes the plot in "Pierre Menard" is openly *textual*. The character is literally a textual construct: he reads texts, he produces
texts, he is made up of texts. In his prologue to *Ficciones*, Borges
writes, "The list of writings I attribute to [Menard] is not too
amusing, but neither is it arbitrary; it constitutes a diagram of his
mental history" (F 15). In "Pierre Menard" there is not a single
physical detail, however circumstantial. As the narrator slyly points
out: "I also had the secondary intention of sketching a personal
portrait of Pierre Menard. But how could I dare to compete with the
golden pages which, I am told, the Baroness de Bacourt is preparing
or with the delicate and punctual pencil of Carolus Hourcade?"
(L 39).

Although Pierre Menard supposedly centers this story, he never
embodies a situation, as does, according to Borges, Hawthorne's
Wakefield. This in itself is not new for Borges. In the earlier stories,
characters were deceptively composed, or fragmented, or shielded
by masks, or, like Evaristo Carriego, deliberately chosen for their
insignificance. Submitted to a circuitous process of characterization, they were momentarily alluded to, then replaced with other,
equally tenuous constructs. However, one did not find a situation
like that of "Pierre Menard," a priori impossible to *embody*, brazenly
pointing out to its exclusively textual make-up.

One approaches the dead Pierre Menard indirectly, through a
narrator evoking the much "lamented poet" as a frequent guest of
the Countess of Bacourt, "before his final monument, amidst the
lugubrious cypresses" (L 36). The tone, anticipating other pompous
hommes de lettres in Borges (Carlos Argentino Daneri, Gervasio
Montenegro), effortlessly establishes the verisimilitude of the narrated character: a second-rate, laborious French Symbolist poet,
possibly pretentious, incorrigibly provincial. Yet Pierre Menard's
bibliography categorically undermines that initial perception. If
some of its entries seem to confirm it, others obstruct it, alienating
Pierre Menard beyond recognition. The stuffy Nîmes poet has foreseeably authored a sonnet sequence for the Baroness of Bacourt; a

transposition into alexandrines of *Le cimetière marin*; a celebratory "portrait" of the Countess of Bagnoregio in a "victorious volume" (published by the very same Countess), which also includes a collaboration by D'Annunzio; a sonnet that appeared twice (with variations) in a Symbolist review, *La Conque*, and a manuscript list of verses that owe their effectiveness to punctuation. Yet Menard also turns out to be, unexpectedly, the author of a monograph on the possibility of building a poetic vocabulary in which there would only be "ideal objects created according to convention and essentially designed to satisfy poetic needs" (L 36); of a monograph on the philosophy of John Wilkins; and of a discussion on the Eleatic aporias. These three topics, apparently alien to the work of a Symbolist poet from Nîmes, are three of Borges's favorite subjects, on which he had already written when "Pierre Menard" was published or on which he would subsequently write.

If the pattern of Menard's mental history is to be found in his heterogeneous bibliography, splitting it into merely two lines—one mocking, the other "serious"—and isolating the elements that constitute each of them, will certainly not do him justice. The author's "visible" work, comprised in this bibliography, is *not*, as the narrator pretends, "easily and briefly enumerated" (L 36). As so many other series in Borges, this one is triggered not only by contrast but by the tension of the inevitably disquieting juxtaposition of multiple, disparate elements, elements not only disordered but virtually *beyond order*. The series is not exactly arbitrary, as Borges claims in his prologue, but neither is it backed by an authority that would justify it. There is no criterion that would allow its reordering, or the establishment of hierarchies among its parts. And yet, defiantly, the series *is there*, to be read in its entirety. It should be remembered that the bibliography appears as a set of *pieces* and that Menard once wrote an article "on the possibility of improving the game of chess, eliminating one of the rook's pawns. Menard proposes, recommends, discusses and finally rejects this innovation" (L 37). All the pieces listed in Menard's bibliography, like the pieces in chess, like the *pieces* in any text, as dispensable as they might seem, carry out their function. To suppress one of them or to try somehow to relocate it in the series represents neither gain nor loss. It does represent an innovation: a new series, another text.

"The list of writings I attribute to him is not too amusing"

(F 15), writes Borges solemnly. But of course it *is* amusing. In a feast of mixed allusions, erudite references, and private jokes, naturalized by the text, the bibliography combines the uncombinable. Although it might be tempting to decode these allusions extratextually, there is *no ground* for such decoding; nor does the cultural nostalgia voiced by Jean Wahl—"It is necessary to know all of literature and all of philosophy to decipher the work of Borges"[2]— seem pertinent here. Pierre Menard's bibliography unquestionably functions like other series in Borges (understanding "series" to signify, more than mere enumeration, the very structure of Borges's text): it proposes the partial recognition of elements in an equally partial series of elements. In the same way that the narrator presents a Pierre Menard whom he patchily recognizes in the fragments of his visible and *invisible* works, the reader carries out a no less erratic task, consolidating his own recognition in partial, parceled elements. It is not necessary to know all of literature or philosophy to decipher the work of Borges, simply because his work does not ask to be deciphered. On the contrary, it offers the reader, if not fleeting identities (like the life of Evaristo Carriego for Borges) then momentary coincidences, coincidences not necessarily willed by the author but recognized, chosen by the reader.

The mental diagram that appears in Pierre Menard's informative, and ultimately disquieting parody of a bibliography hardly allows the reader to shape him out as a character. It is one thing to combine those elements; another, to give them a face. The task should be left to the critics of Tlön who are in the habit of inventing authors: "they select two dissimilar works—the *Tao Te Ching* and the *1001 Nights*, say—attribute them to the same writer and then determine most scrupulously the psychology of this interesting *homme de lettres . . .*" (L 13). In the case of "Pierre Menard, Author of the *Quixote*," imagining the interesting scholar on the basis of his work is as difficult, if not more so, than combining, in a single image (as in the description by Gabriel Miró scorned by Borges) type X feet, type Y throat, and type Z cheeks. But then, the purpose of the text is less to unify than to deliberately dislocate. Menard's restless bibliography is in perpetual tension, affecting the rest of the blurry characters, and tainting them with its mocking ambiguity. The *poet* from Nîmes, called a *novelist* in the first line of the text, is a *mediocre* writer who has produced a text vastly *superior* to that of

Cervantes. In the same way, the pompous, vacuous narrator who opens the narrative is the same (or is he?) who at the end of the story, lucidly and with considerably less florid rhetoric, endorses a revolutionary conception of literature, praising Menard for "having enriched, by means of a new technique, the halting and rudimentary art of reading: this new technique is that of the deliberate anachronism and the erroneous attribution" (L 44). The ambivalence brings to mind that of *Bouvard and Pécuchet*, the two characters who, as Borges tells us, start out as "idiots, underrated and abused by the author" (D 138), and end up sharing Flaubert's intolerance for human stupidity. Like *Bouvard and Pécuchet*, "Pierre Menard, Author of the *Quixote*" draws attention to the practice of literature, proposes a lucid reflection on the participants in any act of writing, in any act of reading. Author, narrator, text, and reader shape and are shaped by the text.

The first acknowledged fiction by Borges does more than "prompt us to go through the *Odyssey* as if it were posterior to the *Aeneid* and the book *Le jardin du Centaure* of Madame Henri Bachelier as if it were indeed by Madame Henri Bachelier" (L 44). It prompts us to contemplate the possibility of a virtually nonexistent character, a link among others in the narrative web of motifs. Moreover, it invites us to mistrust a narrator who because of his contradictions is as inconsistent as the character he presents. Character and narrator lose individual stature even as the situation, explicitly defined by texts, gains importance. Surely something happens in "Pierre Menard"—more precisely, something happens *through* "Pierre Menard"—but the story dispenses with univocity and personification, deflecting them. Beyond the nothingness of personality, narrative situation is constituted here by the nothingness of authority. As the story unfolds, the narrator and his subject, corroded by that nothingness, vanish. What occurs in and through "Pierre Menard" is, after all, writing, which, losing its course, like the protagonist of Cervantes's *Quixote*, comes under the charmed tension Blanchot describes in Henry James. Purely textual (but then so was the tension that haunted the reader Alonso Quijano), this tension combines "the reassurance of a preestablished composition and at the same time its opposite: the freedom of creation, the pure *indeterminacy* of a work, testing that work though not reducing it, not depriving it of all the possibilities it contains."[3]

Borges's first avowed fiction makes manifest what earlier stories had announced, what subsequent texts tirelessly declare: that the written letter inscribes a tension, that the act of writing and the act of reading may seem (and possibly are) tautological acts; that, nevertheless, between Cervantes's text and Menard's own, there is an *undetermined* distance that does not reduce but rather expands the previous text by a new act of writing, a new act of reading. As they recover previous texts, as they open themselves to future ones, Borges's texts do not settle; they literally *unsettle* fixity, undermining the literary monument.

Deflected Signs

In "Pierre Menard," an ambiguous message, coded in bibliography and difficult to recognize, circulates between narrator and reader. The deliberate undecidability of Borges's work is often met with defensiveness, even with laughter, albeit of an awkward nature: "That passage from Borges kept me laughing a long time, though not without a certain uneasiness that I found hard to shake off," Foucault writes about "The analytical language of John Wilkins."[4] Yet laughing at Borges, or rather laughing *with* Borges, is rare, as is the awareness that his text may be disturbing. Borges's text has become a solemn, motionless construct, almost invalidated in the name of culture.

This is a curious destiny for a writer who is marginal both by origin and vocation, and whose texts have always demanded distance. From the very beginning, in his early poetry, Borges chooses periphery at the expense of center, and from that *lateral* stance, both vital and literary, writes his works. The topographical place for Borges (if one dare define such a place) would be the vague line dividing the city from the country, a line allowing, on the one hand, for nostalgia of the center and affording, on the other, the free, confident perspective given by distance. (A preference for *edges* is visible in Borges's poetry; he calls his evenings *lateral*; his suburbs, *extreme*. The streets he walks along, "overcome by immortal distances," give onto nothingness, lose themselves in "the deep vision of plain and sky" [OP 17].)

It is worth recalling that Borges demands such marginality

(fully justifying it) for all of Spanish American literature; better yet, for all marginal literatures. Like the Jews and the Irish, Spanish Americans "are outstanding in Western culture, because they act within that culture and, at the same time, do not feel tied to it by any special devotion": "I believe that we Argentines, we South-americans in general, are in a similar situation; we can deal with all the European themes, deal with them without superstition, with an irreverence which can have, and already does have, fortunate consequences" (L 184).

Irreverence is the inevitable consequence of a marginality that is programmatically assumed. To declare oneself marginal, that is to say eccentric, is to speak from the edge, recognizing a center from which, in an act of self-definition, one has swerved deliberately, the better to see it, the better, if need be, to mock it. However, unlike Foucault, few people laugh when reading Borges. The dubious results of that paralyzing respect especially affect Borges's erudition, which, as a fictional device, has its triumphant beginning in "Pierre Menard, Author of the *Quixote*." The calculated unreliability of the story should be warning enough against a vain archeological quest. As the stability of the narrator, the character, and the rewritten text are questioned, so should the erudite quotes and literary allusions. Unfortunately, this is not always the case. Erudition in Borges is read to the letter, as a guarantee of textual authenticity and authority, ignoring its primary function, which is to create uncertainty through laughter, signaling as it does, at the same time, its own falseness and its truth.

All characters in Borges, after Pierre Menard, are evident textual constructs. Like Hamlet, carrying a book whose variable content is unknown to the audience, Borges's characters always appear with a book, a book they read, write, or interpret; a book that they perhaps unwittingly finish, a book in which they themselves may be mere signs. In "The Theologians," Aurelian and John of Pannonia emerge from a reading of the twelfth volume of the *Civitas Dei*. From a page of Croce's *Poesia* comes Droctulft in "The Story of the Warrior and the Captive." From *Martín Fierro* comes "The End," providing a variant of (and a new ending for) José Hernández's poem. Also taking the latter as a pre-text, "The Biography of Tadeo Isidoro Cruz" lifts an episode from the gaucho poem and elaborates on it freely, from a distance. The reversal illustrated by this particular story—in which the sergeant turns into his opposite, the outlaw gaucho—finds an echo in "The House of Asterion," where the Minotaur appears not as Theseus's opponent but as his willing victim. The reversal of fortune of "The End" becomes, in "The House of Asterion," a reversal of texts. Not only in Borges's imaginary Tlön does each book contain its textual opposite: "The House of Asterion" is the countertext of Apollodorus. Borrowed stories continue to underlie Borges's fiction, not only as a timid man's excuse but as functional pre-texts. In addition to setting the narrative situation, they define its participants. Characters are not embodied according to extratextual criteria; they are embodied intertextually, in the plurality of the stories that contain them.

On more than one occasion, paraphrasing Stevenson, Borges has written that any fiction, any character, is made up of words, and that the transcription of reality is one more illusion of so-called realism since "reality is not verbal" (OI 40). For Borges's characters (and even for their author), reading is more than a circumstantial activity, it is an emblematic representation, expressly referring to their own texture. "The certitude that everything has been written negates us or turns us into phantoms" (L 58), writes Borges, who often takes pleasure in citing Leon Bloy's hypothesis: men, fictional or "real," may well be "versicles or words or letters of a magic book, and that incessant book is the only thing in the world: or, rather, it is the world" (OI 120).

In two of his incarnations, the main character in "The Immortal" is a writer: when he is Homer and when he is Joseph Cartaphilus, who transcribes the story. In "The South," Dahlmann is a reader and a librarian; Averroes, in "Averroes' Search," a writer and a translator. In "Deutsches Requiem," Otto Dietrich zur Linde omits from his list the most illustrious of his ancestors, a writer; later, in a concentration camp, he drives the Jewish poet, whose work he knows so well, to suicide because "he had been transformed into the symbol of a detested zone of my soul. I agonized with him, I died with him and somehow I was lost with him" (L 145). In "The Garden of Forking Paths," a scholar who has deciphered a labyrinth made of letters and another character (foreshadowed in that labyrinth) who is both a teacher and a spy confront each other and momentarily are one. Murdering the scholar, the teacher sends out a message, coded in that very murder, that his German superiors successfully decipher and read as he had planned. (In the same story there is, among so many floating motifs, an unexpected reader: in the train taking him to Albert's house, the narrator observes a plausible group, farmers, a war widow, a "wounded and happy" soldier, and then, unexpectedly, "a young boy who was reading with fervor the *Annals* of Tacitus" [L 21].) In "Death and the Compass," two readers face each other: victory belongs to the more complex of the two, Scharlach, not only a reader of Hasidic texts but also the contriver of a sequence of reading for those texts that he imposes on Lönnrot and Lönnrot unsuspectingly follows.

As in the case of Todorov's "narrative men," for whom "narrative equals life,"[5] Borges's characters come to the end of their lives when they come to the end of their reading, that is, to the end of a reading that they have usually carried out reductively and inefficiently. Because of this inefficiency, Lönnrot dies: drawn by a reading that is prompted by his enemy, he misreads the sequence of crimes that lead to his death. In "Averroes' Search," the diligent but unimaginative translator, deprived of a word to which he has no access and oblivious to circumstances that might help him find it, disappears as he interrupts his translation. In "The Garden of Forking Paths," Stephen Albert is so sure of his successful reading of Ts'ui Pen's labyrinth, in which he *knows* that Yu Tsun will be his enemy, that he disregards, as do Lönnrot and Averroes, the exact moment and nature of the act of reading: a confrontation, forever in the present, with a mobile text based on other mobile texts, never congealing. Turning his back on Yu Tsun, Albert reduces his careful deciphering of Ts'ui Pen's labyrinth to one of its many possible situations, which he unwittingly provokes and fixes with his own death. Death, in Borges, is a form of irony. Cutting reductive readings short by putting an end, effectively, to the reader, Borges criticizes the latter's excessive respect for texts wrongly considered quiescent. Death highlights a misguided fidelity that is, after all, a form of readerly inattention.

Deflected Deaths

Inattention to texts equals death. Although the equation does not imply a moral condemnation, it certainly points to the reader's shortcomings. In three of Borges's fictions, "The Secret Miracle," "Theme of the Traitor and the Hero," and "The Other Death," the conjunction between writing (or reading) and death reappears, suggesting radically different denouements. In all three, besides signaling the end of a limited reading, death affords the character the possibility of modifying, or even rewriting, his own death. In all three stories, death is out of kilter, deflected: instead of providing a narrative closure, it marks a nonconclusion, an illusory end. Finally, in all three stories, a text or a textual construct intervenes to prompt that deflection.

"The Secret Miracle" has often been compared to Ambrose Bierce's "An Occurrence at Owl Creek Bridge," and at some point to Conrad Aiken's "Mr. Arcularis." The situation is the same in all three stories: a cut in time, immediately before the death of the main character, dilates the moment of death and allows for the insertion of an out-of-time sequence. There are, of course, differences among the three stories. In the dilated space created just before his death, Bierce's character continues to live as he had before the war, conjuring up reassuring visions of home with a reunited family. In the same illusory space, Aiken's character takes a trip to Europe and embarks on a rather ridiculous flirtation. Instead, Borges's character, a writer, in that same dilated space, *writes*: "Meticulously, motionlessly, secretly, he wrought in time his lofty, invisible labyrinth. He worked the third act over twice. He eliminated certain symbols as over-obvious. . . . Nothing hurried him" (L 94). In short, each one of the characters projects into that temporal break the substance of his own existence. And we do know that for Hladik "aside from a few friendships and many habits, the problematic exercise of literature constituted his life" (L 90).

However, beyond this tenuous similarity, the quality of the three experiences is notably different. Peyton Farquhar and Mr. Arcularis live out their deferred death without realizing it. They live the illusion of continuity, an experience that does not alter their previous life nor signals its apex but is simply one more "slice of life." On the other hand, Hladik knows that the new time in which he lives and writes signals a rupture in habitual time. There is no illusion; there is a miracle. Time does not flow; it stops, as the heavy drop of rain on Hladik's cheek, so that in that gap—circumscribed, out of time, made sacred—he may add something to complete it, an ending, which is also the end of his poem. In his tragicomedy, "[h]e felt that the plot . . . was best contrived to cover up his defects and point up his abilities and held the possibility of allowing him to redeem (symbolically) the meaning of his life" (L 91). In "The Secret Miracle," divine intervention (absent in the stories by Bierce and Aiken, and infrequent in Borges's own) does not lack irony. The secret miracle is more like a pact: if God gives Hladik one more year of life, it is so that he may "finish this drama, which can justify me and justify You" (L 92). Once the miracle is granted, Hladik, "not working for posterity or even for God, whose literary tastes were unknown to him" (L 94), lives in order to write or writes in order to live. In the end he dies as much from a German bullet as from the last verse of *The Enemies*. Reading, writing, and life have become one: Hladik writes his poem and also his death. Yet, altered by his text, he dies a different man.

"Theme of the Traitor and the Hero" carries the equation between writing and life further, engaging in a more complex development of the theme of the written death. In this case, the text not only dilates physical death but forces itself on that death and radically changes its sign. The entire story functions through deferral and interpolation, a strategy evident in the construction of Kilpatrick's death. A narrator (who is also a writer and a reader), influenced by Leibniz and Chesterton, imagines a plot that he might write some day "and which already justifies me somehow" (L 72). Tentatively describing this plot (while, in fact, writing it), this narrator immediately posits a second writer and reader: Ryan, Kilpatrick's great-grandson, who, wishing to write the true biography of his ancestor, ends up writing his counterbiography. Ryan, in turn, *discovers* a third writer and reader: Nolan, the author of an article "on the Swiss *Festspiele*, vast and errant theatrical representations which require thousands of actors and repeat historical episodes in the very cities and mountains where they took place" (L 74), is the first author of a life of Kilpatrick, even though his text was not so much written as it was interpreted by its hero.

There are no physical traces left of Kilpatrick, the subject of this plural narrative effort, as there were no physical traces of Lazarus Morell, "The Dread Redeemer," or of Hakim of Merv, "The Masked Dyer" in *A Universal History of Infamy*. Kilpatrick's grave has been desecrated, his name crossed out in a document. Yet his masks survive: his statue, which "presides over a gray hill amid red marshes"

(L 72), his name mentioned in poems by Browning and Hugo. To these material representations should be added Nolan's invisible work, which contradicts them and ultimately confirms them. A hero turned traitor, Kilpatrick dies rewritten by Nolan. Just as Bogle orders Tichborne's fate in "Tom Castro, the Implausible Impostor," Nolan plots the staging of Kilpatrick's death, but instead of basing the imposture on journalistic reports, he bases it on a set of texts that hurriedly combine fragments from Shakespeare.

Ryan's reading of his ancestor's story seems as misguided as Lönnrot's in "Death and the Compass." The obvious parallelism between the death of Kilpatrick and that of Julius Caesar leads him to "suppose the existence of a secret form of time, a pattern of repeated lines" (L 73). Such a satisfactory parallelism is shattered, however, with the discovery of an element alien to the scheme, an element that plunges Ryan "into other, more inextricable and heterogeneous labyrinths" (L 73). Ryan discovers that the words spoken to Kilpatrick by a beggar are taken from *Macbeth*, and not, as he expected, from *Julius Caesar*. While the substance of the quote in question is not specified, one could assume it is a passage from act 2, scene 2, referring to the awesome inversion of established order, to things *not being what they seem*, to beings *not behaving as they should*: "A falcon, tow'ring in her pride and place, / Was by a mousing owl hawk'd at and kill'd." In Shakespeare, the speech follows the crime; in "Theme of the Traitor and the Hero," the hero-traitor's exchange with the beggar *precedes* Kilpatrick's murder. It is an announcement, not a confirmation of something that has already happened, a signal to the reader and to Ryan that Kilpatrick's life is not what it seems, that it should be read differently.

In "Theme of the Traitor and the Hero," everything and everyone have already been written, and everything and everyone write. "Pierre Menard" was also ostentatiously textual but now Borges insists on much more subtle combinations. Nolan arranges for the traitor Kilpatrick a death that redeems him in the eyes of Ireland, but, unlike Tom Castro, who passively follows the script composed by Bogle, Kilpatrick swears "to take part in the scheme, which gave him the occasion to redeem himself and for which his death would provide the final rubric" (L 74–75). He not only accepts to be reader and actor in Nolan's version but also, as an active collaborator, he allows himself to introduce variants in the text that will coincide with his death: "more than once [he] enriched the text of his judge with improvised acts and words" (L 75).

Nolan's textual stratagem is the rubric at the end of a life, but Kilpatrick's death also rubricates the text. It is no accident that the text recharges the word *rubric*, fully counting on the polysemy of its range. In the broadest sense of the word, text and life rubricate each other in the "two effusions of sudden blood" (L 75) marking the death of Kilpatrick; they also rubricate each other in the text. Rubric: a peculiar and distinctive mark, written in red. Rubric: by extension, a reference to the blood spilled to testify to some truth. Rubric: in the ecclesiastical sense, a direction for the conduct of divine service inserted in liturgical books and printed in red. Rubric: a red-letter entry of a saint's name in the church calendar. Nolan rubricates Kilpatrick's final moments; and Kilpatrick, as a reader taking part in a script that becomes a canonical text—now faithful to the script, now deviating from it—in turn rubricates Nolan's text. Nolan's life of the hero, a red-letter entry in the Irish national calendar, is additionally rubricated by the "hundreds of actors [who] collaborated with the protagonists; the role of some was complex; that of others momentary. The things they did and said endure in the history books, in the impassioned memory of Ireland" (L 75).

Also a participant in that plural rubrication, Ryan "understands that he too forms part of Nolan's plot" (L 75). Having discovered the "truth," he chooses to diverge from his discovery and to elaborate upon it with good cause. The plot hastily written by Nolan is enriched through the variants added by Kilpatrick and the people of Dublin; this new text is enriched by Ryan's discovery of the underside of the plot. Ryan's duplicitous reading—discovering the traitor only to suppress him; exalting the hero whose public glory he decides to confirm—is enriched by the suppositions about the plot made by the first narrator. Finally, the story "Theme of the Traitor and the Hero" further expands with the participation of the reader. A process of dilation that may appear to be gradual and univocal is transformed through the retrospective recuperation of its stages. The process of interpolation in fact begins to work at the end of the story, not at its beginning, like a series that is always proposing a residue, a gap, the possibility of a new rubric.

3

Fragments and Greeds

And as she had—of me—none of those notions which constitute
a person in one's mind, her eyes, which had barely seen me, had
forgotten me.

Marcel Proust, *Within a Budding Grove*

Opposed to this analogy that denies representation by erasing
duality and distance, there is the contrary one that evades or
mocks it by means of the snare of doubling.

Michel Foucault, "This Is Not a Pipe"

The Dissolving of Character: Doubles

Borges's fiction tends to level all narrative elements, and character
is particularly affected by the process. Questioning it as a mimetic
unity, Borges fragments character to the point of anonymity, reducing it to a letter, a sign, one more element in the text. Characters are
rarely *persons*, they are narrative functions. To refer once more to
his essay on Hawthorne, no one character in Borges embodies a
single situation or accounts for the whole text. Character and situation are shifting processes.

The word *situation* should be understood in the sense given to it
by Borges in his prologue to Bioy Casares's *The Invention of Morel*, by
Henry James in his notebooks, and by Maurice Blanchot in his
essay on "The Turn of the Screw" (the essay where, coincidentally,
Blanchot refers to Bioy Casares, James, and Borges), that is, *situation* is the organization of a *narrative sequence*. Later on, Borges will
replace *situation* with another term, *plot*. Already a favorite term
with Stevenson, *plot* is for Borges what *siuzhet* was for the Russian
formalists, that is, a structurally meaningful organization of ele-

ments. It should be made clear, however, that in Borges's stories, *situation* may coincide totally with the plot, or it may coincide partially, with just one of the different levels that cumulatively constitute that plot. Bearing this in mind, one might say that, in Borges's fiction, character and situation routinely coincide; or rather, one may say that the dissolution of a foreseeable character *is* the situation in his stories. The hard, deliberate preciseness of certain terms in Borges's titles—*form, theme, biography, history*—seems to mockingly support that dissolution, by contrast.

Borges's early fictions present a character dispersed through deceptions and masks. However, in spite of that ambiguity and indirection, those stories do have more or less individual characters, however empty they may be. In *A Universal History of Infamy*, there is always a figure, no matter how blurry or carnivalesque, that, potentially at least, could pull the story together. It might be more accurate to say that in those festive biographies and in *Evaristo Carriego* there is the foreshadowing of a central figure who *might* govern the development of the narrative, a figure whose impending emergence or implicit development *could* center the story. Instead, in later fictions, the story is most clearly decentered. There is no one mask, no one face, just as there is no one character, because "no one knows which is the true man and which his idols" (R 86). The dispersed character in these stories acts as an entire cluster of characters, often designated by different names. In "The Theologians," Aurelian and John of Pannonia are the same person (or the same nonentity) in the eyes of God. In "Story of the Warrior and the Captive," Droctulft and the Englishwoman-turned-Indian are two names for the same character: "The obverse and the reverse of the coin are, for God, the same" (L 131). What Schopenhauer says about history may be said of Borges's fiction: "In his book *Parerga und Paralipomena*, Schopenhauer [compares] history to a kaleidoscope, in which the figures, not the pieces of glass, change; and to an eternal and confused tragicomedy in which the roles and masks, but not the actors, change" (OI 58).

The *figures* called Aurelian or John of Pannonia are also made up of the same bits of glass. Yet this evidence, no doubt courted by the story and prepared at each stage, is only bestowed upon the reader at the end. Regardless of whether the story adjusts or not to conventions of verisimilitude, the basic undecidability of literature allows the figures emerging before the reader to be read simultaneously as the same bits of glass *and* as Aurelian and John of Pannonia.

After "Pierre Menard," the explicit references to masks diminish in Borges's fiction, perhaps because by this point the *predicability* of these references is all too obvious. Instead, Borges's fiction calls attention to the possibility that those same bits of glass, while designating one character, may switch places in permutations unexpected by the reader, thus restoring to that character a much needed *unpredicability*. The character, or the collection of fragments composing it, is a metaphor, a "metaphor or simulacrum" (OI 91). The character's development, the *événement* in which he takes part and which constitutes the story's plot, does not depend on his accumulated actions but on the "diverse intonation[s]" (OI 9) given by the narrator to that metaphor.

The two characters in "The Theologians," Aurelian and John of Pannonia, appear to be such a diversely intoned metaphor. The heresies against which they battle are significant: first, the heresy of the Monotones, who believe "that there is nothing which has not been and will not be" (L 119); then, that of the Speculars (also called *Histriones, Simulacra, Forms*), who propose that man and his acts project an inverted image: "that all men are two men and that the real one is the other, the one in heaven" (L 123). Though they may believe that they stray from these temporally or ontologically repetitive heresies, Aurelian and John of Pannonia are, indeed, *both* Monotones *and* Speculars. Monotony and specularity function as dynamic motifs, not so much between one character and his surroundings as between character and character; or rather, between those fragments, at once solidary and contradictory, which make up the character, a character whose name is now Aurelian, now John of Pannonia.

Within the *sameness* of that character, Borges's story insists, of course, on playing with divergence. The unforeseeable becomes the foreseen; necessary predicability becomes uncanny, working against the character. Long ago, John had usurped a topic from Aurelian's specialty. In turn, Aurelian usurps the refutation of the Monotones that was to be written by John: "he resolved to anticipate John of Pannonia and refute the heretics of the Wheel" (L 120). Aurelian foresees John's probable rhetoric, and *so as not to coincide* with that intuition, he opts for its opposite. Thwarting Aurelian's expectations, John's text turns out to be unpredictable and unpredicable; it does not coincide with the refutation foreseen by Aurelian, nor does it coincide with the refutation Aurelian himself writes: "The treatise was limpid, universal; it seemed not to have been written by a concrete person, but by any man or perhaps, by all men" (L 121). The treatise does prove effective, but only from John of Pannonia's viewpoint: it is his text, not Aurelian's, which serves to condemn Euphorbus the heresiarch to the stake.

At this point in "The Theologians," the end seems foreseeable: "The Wheel fell before the Cross, but Aurelian and John of Pannonia continued their secret battle . . . the name of the *other* does not figure once in the many volumes by Aurelian" (L 122). But if narrative predicability—going from the one to the other, from the other to the one, from one and the same to a divided same—is posited by the text, this predicability works independently from the unpredicability that marks Aurelian's actions: while underlying those actions, it does not entirely determine their manifestations. In order to summarize the new heresy of the Speculars, the better to refute it, Aurelian unwittingly resorts to the previous orthodox and efficacious text by John of Pannonia: "Suddenly, a sentence of twenty words came to his mind. He wrote it down, joyfully; immediately afterward, he was troubled by the suspicion that it was the work of another" (L 124). The twenty words written by John of Pannonia to defend orthodoxy, deflected and subverted by their new context, become heretical, now condemning John to the stake. As one who mimics empty gestures, Aurelian will eventually also die by fire, will die the death of the other who is himself: "He was startled one night towards dawn by the sound of rain. He remembered a night in Rome when that minute noise had also startled him. At midday, a lightning set fire to the trees and Aurelian died just as John had" (L 126).

Beyond the Double

The set of contrasts, diversely predictable and unpredictable, that constitutes character in "The Theologians," goes beyond simple specularity, beyond a satisfactory game of doubles. If merely presented as a clever correspondence between opposites, the diptych Aurelian/John of Pannonia would fall within the facile symmetry of the *Doppelgänger*. But a third element challenges the provisional calm of binary parallelisms and contrasts. That third element, which opens up the structure of "The Theologians," taking it beyond the closure of the double, surreptitiously provides the story's paradigmatic structure. The two symmetrical fires putting an end to the journey of Aurelian/John of Pannonia are foretold (and destabilized) by the mention of two previous fires, both leaving a *remnant* that cannot be obliterated, marking the beginning of an incomplete series of multiple possibilities. The conflagration that opens the story—the burning of the library by the Huns—leaves one volume behind:

> [I]n the heart of the fire, amid the ashes, there remained almost intact the twelfth book of the *Civitas Dei*, which relates how in Athens Plato taught that, at the centuries' end, all things will recover their previous state and he in Athens, before the same audience, will teach this same doctrine anew. The text pardoned by the flames enjoyed special veneration and those who read and reread it in that remote province came to forget that the author had only stated this doctrine in order better to refute it. (L 119)

A second fire, in which Euphorbus the heresiarch, a follower of that doctrine, is burnt at the stake, builds on that remnant, takes Augustine's text, previously "pardoned by the flames," one step further by proposing a *continuum* of variants: " 'This has happened and will happen again,' said Euphorbus. 'You are not lighting a pyre, you are lighting a labyrinth of flames. If all the fires I have been were gathered together here, they would not fit on earth and the angels would be blinded. I have said this many times' " (L 121– 22). Likewise, in "Story of the Warrior and the Captive" and "The Life of Tadeo Isidoro Cruz," a third element interferes with the illusion of binary correspondences, determining the course of the story as it dynamically unhinges it. In "Story of the Warrior and the Captive," that third element is constituted by the gaze, at once sympathetic and distant, of the narrator's English grandmother who, it is suggested, might have seen in the blond Indian woman "a monstrous mirror of her own destiny" (L 130). Even if the grandmother's story is left out of the final figure—the two sides of the

coin bringing together the destinies of the barbarian who chose
civilization and the civilized woman who chose barbarism—it is
nonetheless there, on the *edge*, opening the story up to another tale,
adding another variant in the series. The grandmother's story is
potentially written, as an interpolation that upsets the parallelism
between the contrasting, complementary stories presented in the
text.

"The Life of Tadeo Isidoro Cruz" follows a similar pattern
of reciprocal conversion and concealed imbalance. When Cruz
throws down his soldier's cap and goes to the side of the deserter
Martín Fierro, "[h]e understood that the other man was himself"
(A 85). However, the story begins with the "haunting nightmare"
of a third party, Cruz's father (a character interpolated by Borges,
absent in Hernández's poem). We are told that "Nobody ever knew
what he dreamed" (A 81), just as, in "Story of the Warrior and the
Captive," nobody knows the thoughts of the narrator's grandmother. What we *do* know, however, is that Cruz's anonymous
father was killed by government forces in the swamp grass where
he had taken refuge, and it is precisely in that swamp grass that the
destinies of Cruz (his soldier son) and Martín Fierro (the outlaw
hidden in the swamp) are subsequently played out.

In "Story of the Warrior and the Captive," Borges sets up the
contrast between opposing doubles, then blurs the very duality he
has set up by interpolating the presence of the narrator's grandmother: the contrast is subverted retroactively. In "The Life of
Tadeo Isidoro Cruz," the father's nightmare upsets the contrast
between pairs from the beginning of the story, proleptically. But the
precise moment of the two interferences is hardly important. What
matters is to see them as incisions within the narrative, as breaks,
tenuously suggesting the possibility of secondary tales, performing
another function in the story. Their never explicit peculiarity marks
the passage between the two sides of the coin: they are the edge
where they meet, they are the edge separating them.

If explicit masks disappear from Borges's fiction, there is instead a constant process of *distortion*. If doubles persist (a face that is
a mask, a mask that is a face, the one that is the other), it is because
parallelism and contrast no doubt define the organization of most
stories, at a primary level. Repeating time and again that basic
structure, making it manifest, Borges builds his texts on a recogniz-

able, established convention in order to reflect on and remotivate its elements, in order to question that convention through interpolation and divergence. Distortion within parallelism and contrast, such as that in the examples given, is often made patent in Borges by the use of disfigured, *rubricated* faces: written scars, pointing to parallelism even as they subvert it, like the "spiteful" scar crossing the face of the anonymous Englishman in "The Shape of the Sword." In that story, the scar ("the secret story of the scar" [L 67]) is more than a motif; it is the *situation* of the story, the token of a narrative exchange. With the story of his scar, the Englishman succeeds in buying the fields of *La Colorada* from the previous owner, who had until then refused to sell, and succeeds in imposing his story, in *selling it*, to the narrator who, in turn, relates it to us. All along "The Shape of the Sword," the scar works as a signifier that maintains interest in the story, but whose signified remains deliberately disguised. It is only at the end, when the rivals change places, when listener and reader finally understand the distortion carried out by the tale, in which the narrating hero *is* the cowardly victim of the story, that the signified, faded and wasted, is defined. At the end of his story, the anonymous narrator extols his own courage: "From one of the general's collections of arms I tore a cutlass: with that half moon of steel I carved into his face forever a half moon of blood" (L 71). Yet immediately afterward, as he confesses to being not the hero but the informer—thus amending the rubric that had until now guided his tale—he reveals "with a weak gentleness" the inadequacy of the model of reading he has prompted all along, or rather, its literal exhaustion: the angry half moon of blood on his face has now become "an ash-colored scar" (L 67). A similar distortion is at work in "Ibn Hakkan al-Bokhari, Dead in His Labyrinth," in which two characters, or rather two stages of the same character, Ibn Hakkan and Zaid, confront each other. Once the story has run its course, their disfigured faces end up in the same void: "As you now obliterate me, I shall one day obliterate you, wherever you may hide" (A 119).

In sum, confrontation between doubles, in itself, is of scant interest as a key structuring element in the stories of Borges. To state that Aureliano and John, the warrior and the captive, Kilpatrick the traitor and Kilpatrick the hero, the cowardly Pedro Damián and the fearless Pedro Damián, the *Quixote* by Cervantes and the one by Pierre Menard are the two sides of a coin is a mere starting point for a text that strives to go beyond reassuring binary oscillations. In resorting to these conventional pairings, Borges's fiction undermines a narrative organization whose sole organizing principle would be mere contrast. Scattering the elements that seemingly participate in this dualistic mimicry, it perversely takes pleasure in endowing the resulting fragments—shattered characters, truncated actions, isolated texts—with the illusion of dialogue; a dialogue only fleetingly ascribed to two participants, but which is, more profoundly, multiple.

Lack of Symmetry: Contamination and the Illusion of Desire

More than the complementary contrast between two deceptively unique participants in a dialogue, what matters in these parallels is their final lack of symmetry. The secret correspondence between the complementary theologians is weakened by Augustine's volume saved from the flames and by the flames where Euphorbus perishes. In other cases, parity is disturbed by the emphasis with which Borges privileges one of the two elements over the other. It could be argued that if the text were merely a presentation of parallels, there would be no story; or that there might be a story but the very conventionality of the structure would make it forgettable. While difference, then, is a narrative necessity, what matters is the way in which it manifests itself in the illusory exchange between doubles, and the desire, the craving, that difference awakens. The "coveter of souls" of Borges's early texts and the primitive narrative greed of *A Universal History of Infamy* seem to return, but now desire is not attributed, at least not exclusively, to one character; instead, it operates as a determining motif within the narrative itself. Desire is attributed to (or rather, adheres to) one, then another of the personified fragments that come face to face; once desire is sated, those fragments revert to the same "nothingness of personality," to the same zero degree of desire.

At this zero degree of desire, the possibilities of the unsatiable Aurelian are effectively canceled out. In "The Theologians," the constant shift between presence and absence serves to enhance

Aurelian's presence—one need only recall the wasteful extravagance of Aurelian's first refutation of John of Pannonia—while apparently dooming the other, John, to absence. But as John disappears, so does the craving that kept Aurelian alive, which constituted his very existence: "He felt what a man would feel when rid of an incurable disease that had become a part of his life" (L 126). Cured of his personal desire, Aurelian, in death, becomes a mere symbol, victim of a fire that echoes another fire. He is the obverse and the reverse of John of Pannonia—and of all his others.

Covetousness and greed abound in Borges's characters, in these combinations of narrative elements organized as personalized paradigms, which exert pressure on (and experience desire for) other personalized paradigms. If one leaves the personalizing attributes aside (and indeed Borges's fiction seems to encourage such a move), then covetousness may be seen to determine other aspects of Borges's text. Desire weighs, disruptively, on a text precariously situated between expectation (parallelism, forseeable predicability) and a rupture (unpredicability) that contradicts it. Before abandoning Borges's character, before crossing from a personalized paradigm to a clearly nonpersonalized one, it is worthwhile to take one more look at the personal inflections that Borges attributes to that desire, to examine the coveter and the object of his desire.

"Ibn Hakkan al-Bokhari, Dead in His Labyrinth" contains the clearest (if not the most interesting) example of covetousness. Having stolen Ibn Hakkan's treasure, Zaid realizes "that the treasure was not essential to him. What was essential was that Ibn Hakkan die. He pretended to be Ibn Hakkan, he killed Ibn Hakkan, and in the end he *became* Ibn Hakkan" (A 125). In "Death and the Compass" and "The Dead Man," desire plays a more complex role because its objects are more varied and because, in addition, it is shared. Scharlach, in "Death and the Compass," and Bandeira, in "The Dead Man," lie in wait for the other, leaving a trail rife with decoys; assiduously, they prepare the way for that other who at some point will coincide with them. Equally avid, Lönnrot and Otálora unsuspectingly engage in a path that, although already traced for them, they newly invest with their own desire. In both stories, the final coincidence turns into a double mockery, into a double contamination. The desire, the greed, surging between presence (Lönnrot, Otálora) and absence (Scharlach, Bandeira) is reversible and therefore does not belong to one or the other. As a free-floating element, it settles upon a personalized fragment, then upon another, disrupting the clear give and take between two poles. Desire is neither in Lönnrot-Otálora nor in Scharlach-Bandeira. It simply *is*, disturbing parallelism and complementarity.

The ever-present greed at work in "Death and the Compass" may appear too symmetrical. The mocker mocked and the mocked mocker work after all within a foreseeable, if subversive, framework, that of the detective story as developed by Poe. "The Purloined Letter" is an obvious pre-text and Borges's story acknowledges as much by expressly comparing Lönnrot to Dupin. Both stories are organized around *diverted* signs, or rather, signs *gone amiss*. Dupin and the minister, Scharlach (the true Dupin of "Death and the Compass") and Lönnrot are brothers whose mutual greed cancels them out. However, while Poe's tale sanctions the end of a contract with the mention of an explicit reward, Borges's text does not terminate a pact nor does it cancel covetousness (though it may cancel out the coveters). Above all, it does not cancel the continuation of the story. In quoting Crébillon, Dupin, in "The Purloined Letter," rubricates a story of mutual greed from which his adversary disappears. In "Death and the Compass," Scharlach, revealing the clues that have fed into Lönnrot's desire, seems to do the same. Yet Lönnrot's final statement reopens the text, so to speak, refuelling a ubiquitous, disseminated desire that will never settle. The prospect of Zeno's paradox, forever asymptotic, renews Lönnrot's greed even in death, as it renews Scharlach's, now a killer without a victim, holding on to the dying man's challenge of a future, more difficult, labyrinth in which he, Lönnrot, will never be killed: "The next time I kill you," replied Scharlach, "I promise you that labyrinth, consisting of a single line which is invisible and unceasing" (L 87).

While in "Death and the Compass" desire circulates between coveter and coveted, in a reversible economy that, by the end of the story, becomes clear, "The Dead Man" proposes a less predictable, more complex, *floating* desire at work. The story does not begin with a pretentious detective, but quite simply with a void. The opening lines, not unlike the beginning of *Evaristo Carriego*, promise to fill in that vacancy: "That a man from the outskirts of Buenos Aires, that a sorry hoodlum with little else to his credit than a passion for recklessness, should find his way into that wild stretch of horse country between Brazil and Uruguay and become the leader of a band of smugglers, seems on the face of it impossible" (A 93).

A distorted picaresque (a parodic *Bildungsroman* in a nutshell), "The Dead Man" faithfully lives up to its title and to its opening statement. Benjamín Otálora's life as a leader not only seems impossible, it *is* impossible. Using uncharacteristically abundant physical details, Borges portrays Otálora as a straightforward, sincere figure, all of a piece: "a strapping young man of nineteen [with] a low forehead, candid blue eyes, and that country boy appearance that goes with Basque ancestry" (A 93). Borges also presents, in even more detail, a complex counterfigure, made of scattered pieces, the one that Otálora comes to desire, the one he will want to supplant: "Azevedo Bandeira, though of stocky build, gives the unaccountable impression of being somehow misshapen. In his large face, which seems always to be too close, are the Jew, the Negro, and the Indian; in his bearing, the tiger and the ape. The scar that cuts across his cheek is one ornament more, like his bristling black moustache" (A 94).

The innocent nothingness of Otálora, who has hardly lived, confronts something "misshapen" (the simulacrum, the coherent monstrosity that is Azevedo Bandeira) that is "always too close." A fight seals that excessive proximity. Otálora stops the low thrust of a gaucho's knife aimed at Bandeira; the next day Bandeira sends for him and "praises him up and down, offers him a shot of rum, tells him he has the makings of a man of guts." Otálora becomes one of "Bandeira's men" (A 95). It is no accident that the gaucho who takes Otálora to meet Bandeira is the same one who had tried to knife him, the traitor of the previous night. Otálora remembers that Bandeira does not immediately punish the traitorous gaucho: he "had seated him at his right hand and forced him to go on drinking" (A 95). Yet Otálora does not register this detail, leaving it aside for the reader, for whom it functions as a fissure, as the promise of a *mise-en-abîme*.

The nearness of the misshapen other opens and closes this story. Between those two points comes Otálora's *adventure*, an adventure whose details the narrator claims not to know and which he merely summarizes, resorting to "naturalizing" details, for example, the mention of Otálora's memory kept alive by his old neighbors of Balvanera: "Of the details of his adventure I know little; should I ever be given the facts, I shall correct and expand these pages" (A 93). The vague adventure of "The Dead Man" is not assured by biographical details but by the tension established between proximity and distance. After the first contact with the misshapen, always-too-close Bandeira, Otálora tears up the letter of recommendation he brings for him—an ironically pathetic decision—"preferring to be under no one's obligation" (A 94). He comes to be one of Bandeira's men. He comes to "a new kind of life," although that life, perhaps like Bandeira himself, "is already in his blood" (A 95). This "already in his blood," while providing verisimilitude on a primary level, functions as a *remnant*, disturbing the double Otálora-Bandeira by bringing in, however surreptitiously, the narrator himself: "it is already in his blood, for just as the men of certain countries worship and feel the call of the sea, we Argentines in turn (including the man who weaves these symbols) yearn for the boundless plains that ring under a horse's hooves" (A 95; my emphasis).

Otálora's new life implies distancing himself physically from Bandeira. During those apprenticeship years he sees the other man only once, "but he has him always in mind because to be one of Bandeira's men is to be looked up to and feared, and because after any feat or hard job the gauchos always say Bandeira does it better" (A 95). Public opinion and gossip effectively replace Bandeira's physical presence, doubly stimulating Otálora's greed. This secondhand information, conjuring up for the apprentice the image of the master, on the one hand proposes a limit to be overcome, a specific challenge: to outdo, to be better than Bandeira. On the other hand, the same gossip blurs limits, uncovering a vague space beneath the name Bandeira, a space open to myth: "Somebody has it that Bandeira was born on the Brazilian side of the Cuareim, in Rio Grande do Sul; this, which should lower him in Otálora's eyes, somehow—with its suggestion of dense forests and of marshes and of inextricable and almost endless distances—only adds to him" (A 95–96).

These narrative imprecisions, these cracks discovered by Otálora in the misshapen figure of his master, add to Bandeira, and at the same time render him unstable, turning him into a hybrid. As

Borges describes him in the epilogue to *The Aleph*, Bandeira is "a crude divinity, a half-breed, native version of Chesterton's incomparable Sunday" (AL 171). It is these cracks perceived by Otálora, that allow for his projection into Bandeira's image, a projection based on intuited gaps, on the illusory decline of Bandeira, on "his exhaustion, his weakness, the deep wrinkles of his years" (A 96). Otálora covets the other man's power: "It angers him to be mastered by this old man" (A 96). He covets the other man's sexuality: Bandeira's woman, barely seen during the first encounter between Otálora and Bandeira, takes on new life as Otálora notices her, significantly, as a reflection: "At this moment, he glimpses in the mirror that someone has come in. It's the woman with the red hair; she is barefoot and only half-dressed, and looks at him with cold curiosity" (A 96).

Otálora's greed is so pure in its intensity that it overlooks warning signs, just as he overlooked, as a novice, that Bandeira sat a traitor on his right. Thus the rumor that "an outsider turned gaucho . . . [was] giving too many orders" (A 97), instead of alarming Otálora, flatters him; he misreads it as a harmless joke. His city boy's greed leads him to focus solely on the flashy antithesis of his urban misery, on "a black-legged bay horse that Azevedo Bandeira brings from the south, and that carries a fine saddle worked with silver and a saddle-blanket trimmed with jaguar skin. This spirited horse is a token of Bandeira's authority and for this reason is coveted by the young man, who comes also—with a desire bordering on spite—to hunger for the woman with the shining hair" (A 97–98).

"The woman, the saddle, and the bay horse are attributes or trappings of a man he [Otálora] aspires to bring down," the narrator adds disingenuously. Mindful of these attributes, that is, of the predicability of the character he intends to supplant, the greedy Otálora neglects the *subject* of that predicate. Thus he returns after a shootout, a wounded usurper, "on the boss's horse," and "that evening some drops of his blood stain the jaguar skin, and that night he sleeps with the woman with the shining hair" (A 98). The machinations of greed are seldom so clearly presented in Borges; compared to this story, "Ibn Hakkan al-Bokhari, Dead in His Labyrinth" is a simple exercise in cupidity.

Like Lönnrot in "Death and the Compass," Otálora dies in a trap prepared by someone who is (and the adverb should be taken

literally) *"nominally* the boss" (A 98; my emphasis). However, unlike "Death and the Compass," where death opens a new beginning, "The Dead Man," perhaps because of the coveter's naive
desire to consume the other in order to supplant him, leads to death
and definitive closure. And yet there remains, as a sort of *negative* of
the story, as an inverted supplement, the woman, the saddle, and
the bay horse: attributes or adjectives belonging to Bandeira, they
have become unpredictable because they have been contaminated
by Otálora. Between the clumsily greedy young man who desires
another and the misshapen other who avidly traps the ingenuous
young man, there is a *residue*, a shared, ambiguous predicate that
finally, beyond all binary oppositions, constitutes the story's adventure. At work in "The Dead Man" there is a reciprocal process of
contamination, a mutual blurring.

It may be helpful to recall some of the visual images used by
Borges in other stories to highlight the ubiquity of that multiple
blurring. In "The Dead Man," greed and displacement are constantly highlighted by adjectives that are flashy and red, perhaps
the only ones that Otálora's obtuseness allows him to perceive. In
other stories, greed is deliberately made to coincide with absence of
color, or rather, with borderline color, with the tenuously gray. In
"The Circular Ruins" the gray man with "pale eyes" chooses a place
the color of ashes, "a minimum of visible world" (L 46), in which to
dream up a creature that he will nurture with the "diminutions of
his soul" (L 49). The same *grisaille* is stressed in "Death and the
Compass." When Scharlach intervenes directly in the story, after
indirectly planting the colorful diamond-shaped window panes
as clues for Lönnrot, he masks his face with "a nebulous gray
beard" (L 80). Likewise, in "The Immortal," Joseph Cartaphilus, in
whom several "characters" congregate, is "a wasted and earthen
man, with gray eyes and gray beard, of singularly vague features"
(L 105).

In that faded frontier, like Schopenhauer and Herbart playing
with "ontological multiplication" (OI 19) before him, Borges plays
with narrative multiplication, focusing on the fragmentation of
"character," upsetting complementary, parallel doubles. What
Borges has to say of the *nebulous* subjective hierarchy proposed by
J. W. Dunne, (attractive because it *is* nebulous and thus questions
the subject) is applicable to his fiction, possibly to all fiction: "As to
the consciousness of consciousness that Dunne invokes to establish

in each individual a bewildering and nebulous hierarchy of subjects, or observers, I prefer to suspect that they are successive (or
imaginary) states of the initial subject" (OI 19).

Borges's characters, tensely united by parallelism, contrast, dis-
equilibrium, and greed, are nothing if not "successive (or imaginary) states of the initial subject." The narrator and the reader also
have a place in that series of states, not as a frame but as a reminder
of the variability of the series, of its possibility of multiplying ten-
sions and relations on more than one level. In "Pierre Menard" the
successive and contradictory states of the narrator are incorporated
into the initial subject. "Theme of the Traitor and the Hero" incorporates into its series the reader or readers. "The Other Death"
includes, as successive states, a series of narrators who "read" the
death of Pedro Damián. If we consider greed as the agent upsetting
the balance between bits of character in Borges, we should note
that the same greed functions, disruptively, between narrator and
character, between character and reader.

Disequilibrium: The Ineffective Character

Greed is not the only stimulus accounting for the tension and
combination of these successive states of the initial subject. Borges's
narrators, like Hawthorne's and Kafka's, often point, with the same
unnerving irony, to their characters' fundamental triviality, to their
inefficiency within the plot in which they participate. Kafka and
Hawthorne, Borges points out, share a common rhetoric, that of
stressing "the protagonist's profound *triviality*, which contrasts with
the magnitude of his perdition and delivers him, even more help-
less, to the Furies" (OI 56). That profound trivialization of characters, achieved by canny rhetoric, is all the more noticeable, and
pleasurably perverse, in stories with strong first-person, nearly voy-
euristic narrators. Funes, endowed with greatness—total memory
and the capacity for infinite enumeration—is pared down to size by
a narrator who would not have us forget that he "was also a kid
from Fray Bentos, with certain incurable limitations" (L 59). Pierre
Menard, arguably the most seductive author in Borges's fiction, is
disparaged by the narrator as a "lamented poet." Carlos Argentino
Daneri, the keeper of the Aleph, is consistently exposed throughout
the story as an affected, middle-brow braggart. Only at the story's

(decentered) center—"I arrive now at the ineffable core of my story. And here begins my despair as a writer" (A 26)—and in the equally decentered postscript, does the narrator suspend his implacable trivialization.

While escaping this trivialization bordering on caricature, Averroes, in "Averroes' Search," proves no more effective. His limitations are made manifest in one specific incident. While aware "that what we seek is often nearby," Averroes resorts to the "idle pleasure" of reading, to its "studious distraction" (L 149) in the hopes of understanding the meaning of the words *tragedy* and *comedy*; yet he is blind to the significance of the children's role-playing outside his window, which might have given him a clue. In an epilogue to the story, enunciated by a strong first person, "the process of a defeat" (L 155) is made clear, a process which, with an additional turn of the screw, incorporates the narrator himself.

This rhetoric of insignificance usually functions in only one direction, from narrator to narratee. In "Averroes' Search," however, the explicit limitations of the narrated subject trivialize the narrator himself. In a sense, it is Averroes—Averroes as subject—who enunciates the narrator:

> I remembered Averroes who, closed within the orb of Islam, could never know the meaning of the terms *tragedy* and *comedy*. I related his case; as I went along, I felt what that god mentioned by Burton must have felt when he tried to create a bull and created a buffalo instead. I felt that the work was mocking me. I felt that Averroes . . . was no more absurd than I. . . . I felt, on the last page, that my narration was a symbol of the man I was as I wrote it and that, in order to compose that narration, I had to be that man, and in order to be that man, I had to compose that narration, and so on to infinity. (L 155)

A parenthesis puts an end to this final declaration of shared incompetence: "(The moment I cease to believe in him, 'Averroes' disappears)" (L 155). So too, of course, does the narrator of the story. Naughts, as Borges says, differ but little.

Fragments and Shadows

In Borges's fiction, these bits and pieces of characters, deceptively unique, deceptively paradigmatic, integrate a series where they alternately come into being or are turned into shadows. The direction of the series is of no importance since this is a series where the notion of *hierarchy* disappears, where the value attributed to beginnings and endings also fades, simply because there is no beginning and no end, rather the perpetual, irritating possibility of multiple combinations. The initiator of a series—say Bartolomé Hidalgo, the precursor of *gauchesca* poetry—is insignificant in himself, and only attains his true measure in the tension between his poetry and that of the poets who came after him. "Hidalgo lives on in the vast improvement his offspring brought to his work. He survives in the work of the others; somehow Hidalgo is those others" (D 14). In the same way, the culmination of a series—say Kafka—instead of closing the series, retroactively creates the stages leading up to it, Kafka's pre-texts, and "[i]n this correlation the identity or plurality of men matters not at all" (OI 108).

In "Kafka and His Precursors," Borges writes, "Kafka's idiosyncrasy, in greater or lesser degree, is present in each of these writings, but if Kafka had not written we would not perceive it; that is to say, it would not exist" (OI 108). Nor could we perceive Hidalgo's idiosyncrasy had his work not been vastly improved by his followers. Kafka and Hidalgo neither *end* nor *begin* a series of variants. They merely signal a temporary pause within a flow, a rhetorical marker.

These textual pauses named Hidalgo, or Kafka, are not very different from the pauses marked by Borges's fictional characters. To dwell on Scharlach, or Bandeira, or Kafka, or Hidalgo, is to allow them to direct a reading, to give them, for a moment, the illusion of a personal rhetoric, the doubtful originality of a proper name. The pause in which they are fixed is a passing conceit, the necessary frivolity of an author of fiction, or of history. For instance, when considering the monumental importance of Rosas in the brief history of Argentina, Borges deconstructs the image of the caudillo: "I believe that he was like you and me." Describing him, as if to erase the limits that define the name Rosas, he suggests that, like ourselves, he may have been: "A creature of chance interpolated into action, / who lived out the everyday anguish of things, / and for better or for worse troubled / the uncertainty of others" (OP 37).

What Borges saw as an encouraging possibility in his reading of Hudson—to take on other lives, to enrich oneself with unique destinies, "to broaden the 'I' into a multitude"—has now changed signs. Borges's characters neither allow the reader to take on their lives nor do they broaden the "I" into a multitude. The trajectory is clear: from the tenuous voyeurism of Borges's reading of Hudson, already undermined by the intuition of "the nothingness of personality," to the obvious masks of *A Universal History of Infamy*; then from those masks to their obvious and confused undersides, the partial deceptions, the deficient impostures "where no one knows which is which"; from those impostures to the blurry confrontation of *more or less* complementary opposites; from the temporary satisfaction of the binary to the suspicion, and the eerie manifestation of an *other* or of an equally disturbing *otherness* that has no need for masks. The "I," nothingness, and the other are changeable elements pointing to the same variable interstice. In "Ibn Hakkan al-Bokhari, Dead in His Labyrinth," Zaid kills Ibn Hakkan in order to become Ibn Hakkan; he ends up a vagrant who, in his nothingness, tries to be the other: "He was a good-for-nothing who, before becoming a nobody in death, wanted one day to look back on having been a king, or having been taken for a king" (A 125). This emptiness hungering for a script recalls the vacancy/vagrancy of another loose signifier, Poe's purloined letter. Indeed, Lacan's question, "what remains of a signifier when it has no more signification?" echoes in the disillusioned testimony of the narrator in "The Immortal": "No one is anyone, one single immortal man is all men. Like Cornelius Agrippa, I am god, I am hero, I am philosopher, I am demon and I am world, which is a tedious way of saying that I do not exist" (L 115).

Conceived in this way, the character in Borges is little more than a prop, a deconstructed support. Diminished in its functions, it is "reduced to a mere *trompe-l'oeil*, it is a surviving, incidental support."[1] *Trompe-l'oeil* indeed chacacterizes all of Borges's work, not only his fiction; or rather, to borrow a felicitous phrase, it would be more apt in his case to speak of *trompe-raison*.[2]

4

Postulating a Reality,

Selecting a Reality

Two things are necessary in any neighbourhood where we propose to spend a life: a desert and some living water. . . . A great
prospect is desirable, but the want may be otherwise supplied;
even greatness can be found on the small scale; for the mind and
the eye measure differently.

> Robert Louis Stevenson, "The Ideal House"

At times some birds, a horse, have saved the ruins of an amphi-
theater.

> Jorge Luis Borges, "Tlön, Uqbar, Orbis Tertius"

Reality and Residue

So far I have stressed the deliberate fragmentation of Borges's text:
shattering of character, continuous divergence from the expected,
inclination to disperse the text, to bifurcate it and multiply it, so that
it does not congeal into a rigid set of signs. However, working
against this fragmentation—as if to disturb it, in turn—there remains in Borges's text the longing to fix a created reality. Borges
perversely faults Henry James's fiction for what is, in fact, the
organizing principle of his own: "I believe that his characters hardly
exist outside the story. I believe that his characters are not real"
(Burgin 70). Contrasting James's characters with the "real" characters in Dickens and Conrad, he adds that "Billy Budd is a real man"
(Burgin 78). The Borges who, reading Hudson, admired "lives . . .
as episodic and as real as those invented by God" (TE 35) returns in

these statements. Before analyzing the elusive reality that Borges speaks of, it should be pointed out that this criterium of reality, of a personified reality, is not limited to fictional characterization.

On the one hand, Borges demands for literature and its scribes "an ecumenical, impersonal perception" (OI 12–13). For that reason, he praises the Valéry who proposed a history of literature without a single author's name as "a man who transcends the differential traits of the self and of whom we can say, like William Hazlitt of Shakespeare, 'He is nothing in himself' " (OI 74). For that reason he also praises the nothingness of Shakespeare—"There was no one in him" (L 248)—no different, finally, from the narrator in "The Immortal": both are "Everything and Nothing." Yet on the other hand, disregarding the impersonality of literature, Borges often rescues those "differential traits of the self" and applies them to the most unlikely authors, endowing them with personal attributes, attempting to recuperate the ever elusive reality of the man behind a particular style: "[T]o think about the work of Flaubert is to think of Flaubert, the anxious and diligent worker tirelessly looking up references, producing inextricable drafts. Quixote and Sancho are more real than the Spanish soldier who invented them, but not a single one of Flaubert's creatures is as real as Flaubert" (D 149).

There is some irony, of course, in calling attention to differential, residual traits in order to evoke a writer intent on erasing all trace of authority from his voice, all personal inflection from his work. Borges reacts to Pascal, whose rejection of the self hardly bears mention, in a similar way. He reads Pascal's *Pensées* less as a philosophical reflection than as "traits or epithets" of their author: "the definition '*roseau pensant*' does not help us to understand men but to understand one man, Pascal" (OI 93). *Roseau pensant* is construed by Borges (much to the reader's surprise) as a differential trait of Pascal himself.

When it no longer refers to an individual, or to the self, this residual trait, this differential supplement, is harder to trace. Any attempt to pinpoint it in the text itself might lead one to establish a single stable pattern for the supplement to function, which would in fact cancel the effective mobility of that supplement and restrict the reading of the text. The supplementary trait in Borges's text appears before the reader like Lacan's *remainder* in his reading of

"The Purloined Letter": "a *remainder* that no analyst will neglect, trained as he is to retain whatever is significant, without always knowing what to do with it."[1] This differential remainder has a role in the work of Borges. However, it is not easy to describe the direction that it takes, its role in the dynamics of the text, or the level where it is located. Like Lacan's analyst, like the residue itself, the reader *does not always know what to do*: that is to say, does not know how to read that remainder or how to read him or herself.

A reading of "The Postulation of Reality," in *Discusión*, allows for a first approach to the elusive, differential supplement in Borges. One might even say that the entire essay consists of a careful articulation of differences in whose interstices a residue irritatingly persists. At work from the very beginning, this differential trace, necessary for Borges's critical argument, *remains* at each turn of the essay, fluctuating, not entirely recuperable by either text or reader. The first paragraph of "The Postulation of Reality" chooses the tone of his argument, as well as a critical opponent, Croce, with care:

> Hume noted for all time that Berkeley's arguments do not admit the slightest reply and do not produce the slightest conviction. I would like, in order to eliminate Croce's arguments, a no less gracious and mortal sentence. Hume's does not serve my purpose because Croce's diaphanous doctrine has the power of persuasion, if nothing more. Its defect is that it is unmanageable: it serves to cut short a discussion, not to resolve it. (R 30)

Croce's formula, the identity of the esthetic and the expressive, is the basis for the complex, often arbitrary, framework of Borges's essay. But, remarkably, this pre-text quickly disappears from the essay, which also avoids any subsequent mention of Croce. Croce is a mere point of departure, and to some extent, in view of the ultimate development of the essay, a false point of departure, slightly off track. The mention of Croce is left as a residual fragment, never fully recuperated in "The Postulation of Reality," but useful to describe the rhetoric used by Borges to establish his own line of argument. For Borges's argument is also, like Croce's, deceptively "diaphanous," endowed with "the power of persuasion," even "unmanageable"—though, I would argue, not negatively so. All one has to do is follow the essay step by step, slightly scratching its surface, to see that its persuasive mask barely disguises hiatuses, fissures, unattached differential residues, disquieting contaminations among the different segments of the text, all of which undermine the calm self-assurance of the title. What Borges says of Emerson may be said of "The Postulation of Reality": its "style is a simulacrum of succession" (Irby 36).

Borges initiates his argument with a conventional contrast between "classicists" and "romantics," a contrast more strategical than truly critical since it is deliberately removed from any historical context and declared archetypical. This opening gambit, still containing bits of Croce, is followed by a none too diaphanous distinction between the classicist as one who records reality and the romantic as one who tries to express and represent that same reality, a distinction not unworthy of Croce, the defender of "lyric intuition." Reality, or rather the distinction between realities to which the essay alludes, and immediately complicates, is never defined: rather, it is merely added to the unaccountable residual fragments that gradually accrue in the essay. The supposedly "classical" passage from Gibbon, for example, is not without expressiveness: it is the tale of "prodigious events to whose posthumous allusion [the author] invites us" (R 31). The passage from Cervantes that follows, as another example of the classical mode, obviously contradicts what it is supposed to illustrate. In the scene between Lotario and Camila, the "classical" mode is hardly present; that it be given as an example of the classical, as defined by Borges, defies our understanding, given the very evident process of metaphorization to which Cervantes resorts.

The real supplement in the essay, the differential and unexplainable residue as such, is to be found (decentered, like the revelation of the Aleph) in an inserted hypothesis. The interpolation deliberately cancels out the mock disquisition between classicists and romantics that precedes it and ironically undermines the classifications that follow. Instead, it celebrates two constants of Borges's text, imprecision and selection:

> I would suggest this hypothesis: imprecision is tolerable or plausible in literature because we are always inclined to it in reality. The conceptual simplification of complex states is often an instantaneous operation. The very act of perceiving, of heeding, is of a selective order: every attention, every fixation of our conscience, implies a deliberate omission of that which is uninteresting. (R 31)

Imprecision and selection are at the basis of Borges's problematic postulation of reality, a reality posited solely in the text but not ignoring the projections or contaminations of the "other" reality, the one exceeding the text, with which it engages in a playful counterpoint. If literature may be seen as a finite model of an infinite world, one might add that the work of Borges, through imprecision and selection, through that differential supplement that remains in a sort of inquisitorial function, attempts to incorporate the infinity of the world or its *specular illusion* into a finite model that is perpetually undermined. Nothing less is achieved by the three methods of postulating reality that Borges outlines in his essay in questionable hierarchical order; methods which, he claims, are "classical," that is, denotative and not connotative. Leaving aside his argument against Croce (Borges and Croce: in this instance, striking incarnations of John of Pannonia and Aurelian), these three manners of postulating reality are as much "classical" as they are "romantic," resorting as much to denotation as to connotation. But finally it matters little whether a text record reality or express reality, whether it be "classical" or "romantic." What matters here is the way imprecision and selection are brought into play, in diverse combinations, to characterize the different methods of postulating reality. Indeed, the tenuous difference set up by Borges between reading a "classical" text and reading a "romantic" text fails to convince: "The reality that classical writers propose is a matter of confidence, like the paternity of a certain character of the *Lehrjahre*. The reality which the romantics attempt to exhaust resorts instead to imposition: their constant method is that of emphasis, the partial lie" (R 32). Confidence and imposition, trust and authority, do not differ a great deal, particularly when linked to the concept of paternity. It would be more accurate to say that the ways of encoding reality proposed by Borges rely as much on the confidence of the reader (who accepts imprecisions) as on the imposition of an author who counts on that preestablished trust to decide on the selection of the text, to choose its emphases and its partial lies.

Three Postulations of Reality

The first mode of postulating reality, to which Borges attributes little importance, "consists of a general imparting of the important facts" (R 32). The second consists of "imagining a more complex reality than the one stated to the reader and recounting its derivations and effects" (R 32). The third practices "circumstantial invention" (R 33). Even a cursory look at these methods will baffle the reader, since all three may be ultimately reduced to the first formula: "a general imparting of the important facts." The difference is not so much a question of quality as it is of degree or, more precisely, of emphasis. If the first method does not interest Borges particularly, it may well be because it is, in his words, a *general* account in which everything seems to carry the same weight. If Borges lingers on the commentary of the next two methods, it is no doubt because they suggest, in varying degrees, the possibility of a *particular* account, allowing the differential supplement to function in the story. Because of its power to amaze or because of its elegance (the two are usually synonymous in Borges), such a particular account of reality ultimately coincides, for Borges, with "the important facts." The account of the particular holds up a reality that is essentially a literary reality; a reality incorporating into the text its very extratextuality, synonymous with verisimilitude and literary efficacy.

Of the two modes of postulating a particular reality that Borges prefers in this essay, the first one, recounting the derivations and effects of a reality more complex than the one stated to the reader, would seem to have a particular effect on the periphery of the narrative text or, more precisely, its framing. The reality proposed by this method is not merely based on description: "it often functions on the basis of pure syntax, pure verbal dexterity" (R 33). One should add: on the basis of differential traits, of syntactic residue questioning the organization and concatenation of the text. So it is, in Borges's example, with Tennyson's "so," the adverb devoid of any referent, textual or extratextual, that opens *Morte d'Arthur*. It mimics a nonexistent causality, referring the reader, if not to effects, certainly to derivations that "precede" the poem and thus erase its beginning. In the same way, the use of euphemism, transforming King Arthur's mortal wound into a simple causal, incidental phrase—"because his wound was deep"—blurs (or swerves from) the direct, factual exposition of an event.

The texts chosen by Borges to illustrate his second method, the above-mentioned poem by Tennyson and *The Life and Death of Jason* by William Morris, also resort to what he calls "the unexpected addition" (R 32). Here the postulation of a "larger" reality is not so much based on syntactical resourcefulness or verbal dexterity as it is on manifest expansions. The unexpected addition that Borges selects as an example in Tennyson's poem comes at the very end of the heroic sequence: "and the moon was full." The unexpected addition in Morris's poem, also at the end, is no doubt of a more complex nature: ". . . so what might tell the tale, / Unless the wind should tell it, or the bird / Who from the reed these things had seen and heard?" And Borges adds: "This final testimony from beings who have not even been previously mentioned is what concerns us at this point" (R 33).

These new examples may be classified as syntactical derivations in a broader sense. While their effect may not immediately affect textual syntax, they certainly affect the narrative *grammar* of the stories, not just because of their semantic content but fundamentally because of their intrusion (no less surprising than Tennyson's "so" or "because") in a passage the reader considered closed. In all fairness, however, it should be pointed out that the semantic content of these two additions does allow for a greater possibility of "imagining a more complex reality than the one stated to the reader and then recounting its derivations and effects," than the "so" and "because" examples cited previously, which are of an exclusively syntactical nature.

In the description of this method, "a more complex reality than the one stated to the reader" does not presuppose an extratextual reality. On the contrary, given the nature of the examples given, "a more complex reality" is itself textual. The differential traces observed by Borges are potential points of departure for oblique narratives, for what Stevenson, on reading Jules Verne's *L'Ile mystérieuse*, called "surprise[s] that I had expected": "[W]hole vistas of secondary stories, besides the one in hand, radiated forth from that discovery, as they radiate from a striking particular in life: and I was made for the moment as happy as a reader has a right to be."[2]

Similarly, in Borges, certain syntactical surprises, insertions appearing to be trivial, obliquely open up the story. Think, for example, of the narrator's surprisingly personal intervention in "The Lottery in Babylon": "I don't have much time left; they tell us that the ship is about to weigh anchor" (L 33); or the provocative parenthesis interrupting Yu Tsun's list as he goes through his pockets in "The Garden of Forking Paths" and finds a letter "which I resolved to destroy immediately (and which I did not destroy)" (L 20–21); or the use of a demonstrative in "The Waiting": an "Uruguayan twenty-centavo piece which had been in his pocket since *that* night in the hotel at Melo" (L 165; my emphasis); or the unexpected apostrophe in a descriptive passage of "The Library of Babel": "You who read me, are you sure of understanding my language?" (L 58).

The third mode of postulating reality proposed by Borges, "the most difficult and most efficient" of the three, resorts to circumstantial invention. Examining a banquet scene from Enrique Larreta's *La gloria de Don Ramiro*, Borges dwells on the felicitous detail of a padlocked tureen: "[T]hat spectacular 'bacon broth, served in a tureen with a padlock to defend it from the voracity of the pages,' [is] so suggestive of genteel poverty, of the string of servants, of the big old house full of stairs and turns and different lights" (R 33).

The "suggestive" charge attributed to this detail by Borges, and his subsequent fanciful elaboration would seem to reduce this method to a simple variant of the previous one. This is not exactly the case. It must be remembered that the three modes of postulating reality are three diverse intonations of the same basic intention: to set down the "important facts." The three modes function like a set of Chinese boxes, and if the third method differs from the one preceding it, the difference is not so much a question of perspective as it is (Borges's attacks on the romantics notwithstanding) a question of emphasis.

The second method proposed by Borges, setting down the derivations of a more complex reality than the one stated to the reader, relies on literary suggestion, on the blurring of limits. It tempts the reader with the illusion of what has not been said, with the never explicit promise of new openings, of secondary stories. Instead, the third method proposed by him relies (as all texts do in the long run) on the exposition of "laconic details with long-range consequences" (R 33), and does so through a direct and concretely selective process, within the boundaries, as it were, of the story itself. This last mode is not so different from Barthes's "reality effect":[3] the barometer in *Un coeur simple* is equivalent to the tureen in *La gloria de Don Ramiro*. However, examples of that third method of postulating reality, which Borges so enjoys finding in the works of others, do not abound in his own: there are few *objects* in Borges, no tureens, no barometers. Even as he praises this third mode of postulating reality as the most difficult and the most effective, he deems it "less strictly literary than the two previous ones" (R 33). If Borges resorts to circumstantial invention, he does so in a peculiar manner, having little to do with the invention of objects.

If we compare the last two modes of postulating reality we will see that the difference is, in fact, a difference in emphasis. Compare, for example, the mention of the concrete, particular tureen with the deliberately elusive full moon in the reading of Tennyson proposed by Borges. The mention of the moon would open possibilities toward an "outside," beyond the realm of the written, toward new stories. Instead, the concrete padlock on the tureen would refer back to an "inside," recorded in the text. The methods are obviously reversible, of course; to speak of an "inside" and an "outside" makes little sense since the differential supplement, whether implied or explicitly written, is already in the text.

"Reality is not vague, but our general perception of reality is, and here lies the danger in over-justifying actions or inventing numerous details" (Cozarinsky 30), writes Borges, observing, of that same reality, that it cannot be transcribed. "The Postulation of Reality" may be described as a perplexed (and perplexing) inquiry into the exercise of verbal mimicry, that is, into the practice of literature. While one of the methods deceitfully suggests a simple denotative mode, the other two resort to connotation, carried out on different levels. Of the latter, one blurs boundaries, rescues possibilities within what James called the "splendid waste"[4] of the real, and mimics a dynamic, vital process; the other, through the precise and select use of circumstantial invention, imitates concrete, "real" details and feigns to "capture" reality.

The ambiguous charge of the word *postulation* is of course disconcerting. To postulate is to request something from another, relying on his *trust*; but to postulate is also to propose, perhaps even to *impose* something on another. In the two methods on which Borges dwells, what is postulated (as a trustful request, as an imposition) is a simulacrum of reality: a term, which this essay by Borges, perhaps not surprisingly, avoids.

The Charm of the Circumstantial

If the tenuously diverse modes of positing reality discussed by Borges are held up to his own stories, one will find bits of all three methods in each. In none of them is there a dominance of *one* of the modes; in all, there is a combination of the three in a dynamic counterpoint. To simplify, one may say that Borges's effectiveness begins, primarily, with an economical (and deceptively denotative) application of the first method he mentions: a general imparting of the important facts. Even this simple approach brings into question the multiple semantic possibilities of the word *facts*. The *actions* through which Emma Zunz constructs herself are facts; so are the *writings* of Pierre Menard, the *readings* in "Theme of the Traitor and the Hero," the unsympathetic *parodying* in "The Aleph" or in "The Zahir." The postulation of reality proposed by Borges is an account of the *important* facts, so that, from the very start, this account is spotty, constituted as much by the highlighted significant as by the erased insignificant. (Stevenson quotes Benjamin Franklin: "As we must account for every idle word, so we must for every idle silence" [71].) If the supposedly denotative quality of Borges's first mode of postulating reality is seriously compromised by the erasures resulting from selection, so that we end up with a process of selective denotation, the next step will be, foreseeably, a process of connotative selection. The second and third modes of postulating reality respond to that connotative inclination: the laconic detail with long-range *syntactic* consequences and the laconic detail with long-range *semantic* consequences splinter an utterance that at the same time seems to relish these interruptions.

Of the three modes described in "The Postulation of Reality," Borges no doubt resorts more to the second, based on syntax. Circumstantial invention, in his work, is less a fact than a longing. Few readers, indeed, seem as delighted as he when finding it in other writers or as open as he to its suggestive charge. The comments he weaves around the locked tureen in *La gloria de Don Ramiro* are but one example. Borges notes that Hawthorne's diaries propose "thousands of trivial impressions, small concrete details (the movement of a hen, the shadow of a branch on the wall); they fill six volumes and their inexplicable abundance is the consternation of all his biographers" (OI 63). Seeing circumstantial invention at work in those details, he adds: "I believe that Nathaniel Hawthorne recorded those trivialities over the years to prove to himself that he was real, to free himself, somehow, from the impression of unreality, of ghostliness, that usually visited him" (OI 63).

Quoting Gibbon, Borges recalls in *Evaristo Carriego* that "the pathetic, almost always, consists in the detail of little circumstances" (EC 41). He returns to that notion in his essay on "La poesía gauchesca," speaking of "instances of the pathetic" (D 36) in one stanza of the poem *Martín Fierro*:

> There was a little gringo captive,
> always talking about his ship,
> and they drowned him in a pond
> for being the cause of the plague. . . .
> His eyes were pale blue
> like a wall-eyed foal.[5]

Borges is aware of the different pathetic projections of this stanza. The obvious ones outline a secondary story: "atrocity and pointlessness of that death, the plausible memory of the ship, the odd fact that a boy who crossed the seas safely should drown in the pampas" (D 36). Yet Borges prefers the circumstance that adds nothing to the dynamic possibilities of that secondary story: "[T]he stanza's greatest power lies in the postscript, memory's pathetic addendum: *His eyes were pale blue / like a wall-eyed foal*, so typical of someone who, considering the story closed, is presented by memory with one more image" (D 36). This one more image, perhaps at first glance insignificant, is nevertheless the one Borges retains, for the sheer pleasure of it, as he rereads Hernández's text. A detail in fact less "pathetic" than the situation recounted in the stanza (a foreigner made responsible for an epidemic, a sailor drowned in a shallow pond), an image that does not open up a new story, the mention of the English boy's blue eyes is retained as a pure differential supplement: it is just *one more image*.

Stevenson as Precursor

"The charm of circumstance": the phrase could be Borges's but it belongs to Stevenson, a writer who figures prominently in Borges's brief list "of authors whom I continually reread" (F 106). Stevenson's presence is felt throughout Borges's work, acknowledged in prologues, included in the text itself. Curiously, Stevenson is never *quoted* directly in an oeuvre in which literal quotations are not uncommon. Borges's approach to Stevenson is singularly oblique; its result, difficult to describe. Stevenson is a childhood memory: the blind buccaneer in *Treasure Island*, "dying under the horses' hooves" (EC 33), is one of the characters marking Borges's disquieting first contact with fiction, along with the Veiled Prophet and "the time traveler" from Wells. Years later, Borges returns to the character in the poem "Blind Pew" (DR 72). But Stevenson's influence, of course, is more complex than all that.

Indirect reference to Stevenson, in a text so rich in indirect references, is singularly consistent. By this I mean that the way in which Borges relies on the work of "one of the best loved, most heroic figures in English literature" (ILI 51) is systematic. While there is no direct quotation, there is continuous allusion. The prologue to *A Universal History of Infamy* states that the protofictions composing it derive in part from a rereading of Stevenson. Again Stevenson appears in the prologue Borges writes for Bioy Casares's *The Invention of Morel*, this time as support for a theory of fiction. There are fragments of Stevenson's *Chapter on Dreams* paraphrased in *Other Inquisitions* (OI 15, 139). These are but a few of Borges's references to Stevenson and his work. One more bears mention, since it supports a recurring theme in Borges, the questioning of literary "paternity" and, concomitantly, the questioning of the notion of a fixed text. Borges writes in the preface to the French translation of his poetic works: "In order to judge, today's reader wants to know whom he is dealing with. That is why critics have ignored Stevenson's best novel, *The Wrecker*: the author had written it in collaboration with his son-in-law, Lloyd Osbourne, and no one dared to praise a book of uncertain paternity."[6]

In general, it is not easy to describe the exchange between Borges and the authors he cites; Stevenson is no exception. However the dialogue between Borges's text and an *ever-present* Stevenson, proposes, more than in other cases, a rereading of a new Stevenson. Through two unjustly forgotten essays, "A Gossip on Romance" and "A Humble Remonstrance," Borges creates his precursor. To read Stevenson after having read Borges (an experience similar to reading Kafka's precursors after having read Kafka) is a remarkable exercise in critical *mise-en-abîme*. Borges's deliberately artificial postulation of verisimilitude in fiction, his hesitation before fictional characterization, the indetermination he posits between reader and text, are all already present in this passage from "A Gossip on Romance":

> No art produces illusion; in the theatre we never forget that we are in the theatre; and while we read a story, we sit wavering between two minds, now merely clapping our hands at the merit of the performance, now condescending to take an active part in fancy with the characters. This last is the triumph of romantic storytelling: when the reader consciously plays at being the hero, the scene is a good scene. Now in character-studies the pleasure that we take is critical; we watch, we approve, we smile at incongruities, we are moved to sudden heats of sympathy with courage, suffering or virtue. But the characters are still themselves, they are not us; the more clearly they are depicted, the more widely do they stand away from us, the more imperiously do they thrust us back into our place as a spectator. . . . It is not character but incident that woos us out of our reserve. Something happens as we desire to have it happen to ourselves; some situation, that we have long dallied with in fancy, is realised in the story with enticing and appropriate details. (128)

"The characters are still themselves, they are not us," writes Borges's prescient precursor. At another point in the same essay, he calls characters "puppets . . . [whose] faces are of wood, their bellies filled with bran" (126); in a less truculent mood, he refers to them—with a phrase that Borges will in turn adopt—as verbal objects. In any case he sees them, as does Borges, not as ends in themselves but as vehicles for narration.

Stevenson's "appropriate, tempting details," do not differ from the differential traits that according to Borges, ensure the postulation of reality: on the one hand, the dynamic detail allowing for the "vast visions of secondary tales"; on the other, the static, perhaps trivial detail, the "one more image" that captures the reader. Of the wreck in *Robinson Crusoe* and the heterogeneous nature of the objects he salvages, Stevenson writes that "Every single article the castaway recovers from the hulk is 'a joy for ever' to the man who reads of them. They are the things that should be found, and the bare enumeration stirs the blood" (127).

More than to the enumeration, however arbitrary, of objects, of static detail, Stevenson resorts to dynamic detail to insure the verisimilitude of his fiction. Or rather, he resorts to a dynamic detail that he wilfully suspends and, for a moment, congeals. Unlike writers who choose static detail for its own sake, Stevenson, like Borges, chooses it to suspend action. His goal is not to transform that detail into a sumptuous token, like Larreta's tureen or Flaubert's barometer, but to fix, through reading, through memory, an emblem within a text:

> The threads of a story come from time to time together and make a picture in the web; the characters fall from time to time into some attitude to each other or to nature, which stamps the story home like an illustration. Crusoe recoiling from the footprint, Achilles shouting over against the Trojans, Ulysses bending the great bow, Christian running with his fingers in his ears, these are each culminating moments in the legend and each has been printed on the mind's eye forever. Other things we may forget; we may forget the words, although they are beautiful; we may forget the author's comment, although perhaps it was ingenious and true; but these epoch-making scenes, which put the last mark of truth upon a story and fill up, at one blow, our capacity for sympathetic pleasure, we so adopt into the very bosom of our mind that neither time nor tide can efface or weaken the impression. This, then, is the plastic part of literature: to embody character, thought, or emotion in some act or attitude that shall be remarkably striking in the mind's eye. (123)

The examples given by Stevenson—Crusoe's start, Christian's gesture, Ulysses frozen as he bends his bow—turn the charm of circumstance into a hybrid element. Suddenly, characters who "are not us" fulfill, with a memorable *gesture*, "our capacity for sympathetic enjoyment." In other words, those gestures, besides attesting to literary efficacy, survive in the reader's memory in a peculiar way: as narrative emphases, they serve, as Stevenson says, to "stamp the story home."

The Emphatic Gesture

Emphasis does not seem to be a literary device that as a rule would garner the approval of Borges. He uses the word to condemn Góngora's verses (HE 74), infelicitous phrases by Flaubert (D 48), and in more general terms, to condemn the romantic writers he disdains. His condemnation extends to modern writers; with notorious bad faith, Borges calls emphasis "the preferred error of modern literature":

> Definitive words, words that postulate intuitive or angelical insights, or resolutions of an all too human strength—*only, never, always, all, perfection, completion*—are the stock in trade of *all* writers. They do not realize that to overstate something is as awkward as not to say it entirely, and that careless generalization and emphasis are deficiencies and that the reader perceives them as such. (D 49)

(Incidentally, some of Borges's favorite words—words like *maybe, perhaps, possibly*, used in Borges's text *in order not to say entirely*—are, despite their obliqueness, no less emphatic.)

Before considering how emphasis works in general in Borges's text, we should recall that, like Stevenson in fiction, Borges isolates and emphasizes gestures and attitudes. This occurs in his stories but also in his film reviews. From John Ford's *The Informer*, Borges remembers "the dangling man's fingernails grating on the cornice at the very end and the disappearance of his hand as he is machine-gunned and falls to the ground" (Cozarinsky 31). Discussing Marc Connelly's *Green Pastures*, he notes: "We are amused when God saves the 10¢ cigar, which the Archangel has just offered him 'for later'" (49). In Ozep's version of *The Brothers Karamazov*, he delights in the detail of "Smerdiakov's clerical hand extracting the money" (23). Some stories in *A Universal History of Infamy* also rely on the effectiveness of a detailed gesture or an attitude: Billy the Kid ostentatiously sleeps next to his first victim; Monk Eastman strolls with a blue pigeon on his shoulder. The same focus on gesture may be observed in subsequent fictions to "stamp the story home." In "The End," the story seems to freeze on a scene. After killing Fierro, the black man "wiped his bloodstained knife on the grass and walked back toward the knot of houses slowly, without looking back" (F 162). This gesture that, as Borges writes, "signifies [the gaucho] as a whole" (D 34), echoes a scene from *Martín Fierro* that Borges finds memorable and, at the same time, is its exact opposite: it is the gesture Martín Fierro himself had made after killing the black man's brother.

The gestures and attitudes on which Borges focuses rely on the visual, but not exclusively so. As has been mentioned, Borges's references to the visual, in prologues and interviews, are singularly hazy. In the prologue to *A Universal History of Infamy*, he points out the importance of visual intention in the stories. Nevertheless, in an interview with Georges Charbonnier, he claims not to have much "visual imagination"; he concurs with the interviewer that there are visual elements in "Funes the Memorious" but slyly adds "the smell of maté" to the interviewer's list of visual images.[7] In his conversations with Richard Burgin, he states, at one point, that "the visual element is not very important in my books" (Burgin 70). The obvious biographical reference to blindness, often used by Borges himself, does not really account for such vagaries. By "visual," Borges seems to means what James called "pictorial," an object (or combination) "adorably pictorial,"[8] or what Stevenson rescues with "the mind's eye." "Art—always—requires visible unrealities" (OI 114), writes Borges on the subject of Zeno's paradox: he would like to know, he adds, "the name of the poet who endowed [them] with a hero and a tortoise" (OI 110).

In Borges's text, the visual never implies inertia, but rather a contained force, suspended on a detail, gesture, or attitude that mobilizes the story. The same may be said of any pause, of any moment where Borges's text gives the illusion of settling. These gestures, attitudes, or signs are never inert: there is always change, *incidence*. Furthermore, these gestures that sum up characters and signify them as wholes are not devoid of symbolic projections. The meticulous cleaning of the knife would be a case in point; other examples could be added to show that, as in "The End," a character's gesture often coincides with the recognition of his destiny, that is, with his fundamental otherness. In "Tom Castro, the Implausible Impostor," a gesture seals the pact between Arthur Orton and Bogle as a revelation of mutual insecurity. The empty character looking for an identity recognizes something of himself in the Bogle who is afraid to cross the street: "After studying him for a long while, Orton offered the Negro his arm, and, sharing the same amazement, the two men crossed the harmless street. From that moment of a now dead and lost evening, a protectorate came into being— that of the solid, unsure Negro over the obese dimwit from Wapping" (UHI 32). Similarly, at the end of "The Life of Tadeo Isidoro

Cruz," an unexpected gesture seals the recognition of a different destiny. Realizing that "the other man was himself" (A 85), Cruz throws down his soldier's cap and crosses over to the enemy's side.

These gestures and these attitudes are not the only memorable ones in Borges. More interesting perhaps, in the way they stamp the story home for the reader, are others, apparently small and insignificant. Take, for example, the fleeting image of Herbert Ashe in "Tlön, Uqbar, Orbis Tertius," a story stripped of characters. A creature as gray as his name, who "suffered from unreality" (L 6), he is unforgettably stamped "in the hotel corridor, with a mathematics book in his hand, sometimes looking at the irrecoverable colors of the sky" (L 6). In "Funes the Memorious," perhaps the best example, there are two images of Funes that are difficult to forget. First he is described "with a dark passion flower in his hand, seeing it as no one has ever seen it" (L 59). Then, before the story unfolds through Funes's exceptional memory, he is captured in a vertiginous image:

> It had suddenly got dark; I heard some rapid and almost secret footsteps up above; I raised my eyes and saw a boy running along the narrow and broken path as if it were a narrow and broken wall. I remember his baggy gaucho trousers, his rope-soled shoes, I remember the cigarette in his hard face, against the now limitless storm cloud. Bernardo cried to him unexpectedly, "What time is it, Ireneo?" Without consulting the sky, without stopping, he replied: "It's four minutes to eight, young Bernardo Juan Francisco." His voice was shrill, mocking. (L 60)

The reader of "Funes the Memorious" will remember a story about a man whose memory hoards all things, or rather the infinite variants of all things. But he will also recall both of these circumstantial, unexpectedly satisfying images, seemingly so cut off from the story's subsequent development. One could argue, with some cause, that in a way the two images refer to the *subject* of the story, to the singular perception of time and space later explained by Funes himself. However, what matters is the deliberately isolated presentation of the two images. The story will require a radical break, not too different from the one in "Pierre Menard," for the two memorable images of Funes to stop being charmingly circumstantial and to become significant in another way. The necessary break comes with the accident that cripples Funes's body, denying him the possibility of any gestural representation. Little remains of that first Funes, stamped "in the mind's eye" of the reader. When the narrator visits Funes, immobile in his cot, he notices the same mocking voice, the same cigarette, but the memorable gestures, the charm of circumstance, are missing. The "hard face against the . . . limitless storm cloud" of the beginning becomes, at the end of the story, a vacant, rigid effigy: "he seemed to me as monumental as bronze, more ancient than Egypt, older than the prophecies and the pyramids" (L 66).

Funes's first gestures serve a similar function in this story as the gesture of the Indian Englishwoman in "Story of the Warrior and the Captive." These gestures signify in themselves, and while they may no doubt be made to signify more generally in the economy of the story, to do so reduces their impact as isolated traits. When the first images of Funes are incorporated into the second part of the story, when they become components of a broader paradigm, they lose their individual thrust. Something similar occurs with the memorable gesture of the Indian Englishwoman in "Story of the Warrior and the Captive": "[O]n a ranch, near the sheep dip, a man was slaughtering one of the animals. As if in a dream, the Indian woman passed by on horseback. She threw herself to the ground and drank the warm blood" (L 130). While the gesture in itself "stamps the story home," it is in turn subsumed by the paradigmatic contrast between civilization and barbarism, set forth from the beginning of "Story of the Warrior and the Captive." To disregard the deliberately individual impact of those gestures, diminishing their strangeness, forcing them to signify unequivocally within the story would be reductive. Indeed, if this were done, a single comment by Borges, a gesture he mentions in passing, taken literally, would plunge the reader of the gospels into conceptual confusion. Paraphrasing John, Borges recalls a curious gesture made by Christ, "the greatest of oral teachers": he once wrote "some words on the ground, and no man read what He had written" (OI 117).

Borges's text, like Zeno's paradox, is marked by "periodic abysses" (OI 113). Of the world, he writes that "[w]e have dreamed it resistant, mysterious, visible, ubiquitous in space and secure in time; but we have allowed tenuous, eternal interstices of unreason in its structure so we may know that it is false" (OI 115). Borges's description of the world could be applied to his texts, also riddled with "tenuous interstices," that defy domestication and defeat the reader trying to force them into a rigid, iron-clad meaning. (Such a reader is no different from the one who tries to *decipher* Borges's erudition.) Borges's postulation of narrative reality takes hold in those contingent gaps, in those circumstantial, surprising, often memorable gestures that, more than establishing links, function as *trompe-l'oeil*.

The Waste of the Circumstantial

Failure to recognize the charm of the circumstantial is the basis, in Borges, of an ironic situation. This is especially true in those fictions that contrast the inefficacy of the character with "the magnitude of his perdition" (OI 56), such as "The Dead Man," "Death and the Compass," and "Averroes' Search." In the last two, when the characters are on the verge of completing an incompetent reading that will put an end to their lives, Borges grants them, rather perversely, a renewed attention to circumstantial detail. Before depriving him of his fleeting reality, the narrator of "Averroes' Search" grants his character a trivial gesture, by now useless in the unfolding of his story: "He felt sleepy, he felt somewhat cold. Having unwound his turban, he looked at himself in a metal mirror. I do not know what his eyes saw, because no historian has ever described the forms of his face" (L 155). In the same way, at the end of "Death and the Compass," the narrator allows the diligent Lönnrot to experience the circumstantial. Thinking that he is in charge of the situation, Lönnrot "had very nearly deciphered the problem; mere circumstances, reality (names, prison records, faces, judicial and penal proceedings) hardly interested him now" (L 82). Pathetically sure of himself, he focuses, for the first (and last) time on circumstance. For the first time, before coming face to face with death, he is allowed to *see*: "He saw dogs, he saw a car on a siding, he saw the horizon, he saw a silver-colored horse drinking the crapulous water of a puddle" (L 83). Like Averroes, "he felt somewhat cold." Also as in the other story, his death is accompanied by the now superfluous detail, by the addition of one more image: "[F]rom the dusty garden came the futile cry of a bird" (L 86). The belated recognition of the circumstantial, conveyed all too late to these characters, becomes pathetic. Not only that: it becomes pure waste.

5

Converting the Simulacrum

There are situations and ideas which cannot be envisaged clearly
without our dying of them, or causing someone else to die.

Paul Valéry, *Analects*

The traditional conception of metaphor is perhaps the least impossible of all: to consider it as an ornament. I am aware that this
is a metaphoric definition of metaphor, but it does have its merits.
To speak of ornament is to speak of luxury, and luxury is not as
unjustifiable as we might think. I would define it thus: Luxury is
the visible expression of happiness.

Jorge Luis Borges, "Indagación de la palabra"

Organization and Emphasis:
The Uncanny Distortion

Borges's text is organized as a series of gradual deceptions, similar
to the moves so extravagantly and efficiently displayed in *A Universal History of Infamy*; similar also to the *Thousand and One Nights*, as
read by Borges, where "the antechambers are a confusion of mirrors, the mask is beneath the face, so that no one knows which is
the true man and which his idols" (R 86). "And nothing of that
matters," adds Borges with apparent nonchalance, "that disorder is
trivial and acceptable as the inventions of a man when he first dozes
off into dream" (R 86). He goes on, however, to an unsettling
conjecture: "Chance has played at symmetry, at contrast, at digres-
sion. What would a man, a Kafka, not do to organize, emphasize
those games, reproduce them according to German deformation,
according to the *Unheimlichkeit* of Germany?" (R 86).

This wishful conjecture closes the essay on "The Translators of the Thousand and One Nights." Discussing Littmann's translation, Borges had already noted that "The intercourse between the *Nights* and Germany should have produced something more," adding that "There are marvels in the *Nights* that I would like to see rethought in German" (R 86). Later, in his essay on Beckford's *Vathek*, Borges elaborates on the notion of uncanny "distortion," expanding its German national limits. He links the uncanny to an "abominable hue of brown" that haunted Stevenson in his childhood dreams; to a tree imagined by Chesterton, "a tree which is already more, or less, than a tree"; and to the writings of Poe, Melville, De Quincey, Baudelaire, and Beckford himself (OI 139–40). A good portion of Borges's essay "On Chesterton" is also devoted to a discussion of the uncanny. Observing that Chesterton "tends inevitably to revert to atrocious observations" (OI 83) and that "something in the makeup of his personality leaned toward the nightmarish, something secret, and blind, and central" (OI 84), he sums up Chesterton's uncanniness in a memorable phrase: "He defines the near by the far, and even by the atrocious" (OI 83).

It is hard to know whether Borges's interest in the uncanny refers indirectly to Freud's essay, which predates Borges's by several years. His rare allusions to Freud, mostly unfavorable, would seem to preclude such a possibility. However, even though Borges and Freud consider the consequences of "distortion" in radically different ways, bringing the two together is not entirely impertinent since there are odd similarities in their shared interest in (or rather their passionate curiosity for) the uncanny as an organizing principle. Prompting the uncovering of a barely masked disquiet, the uncanny, as Freud writes quoting Schelling, "is the name for everything that ought to have remained . . . hidden and secret and has become visible";[1] it is based on, even as it battles with, the *uncertainty* of its "distortions." After all *unheimlich*, as Freud points out, is not the opposite of *heimlich*, but often its synonym: the disquieting unfamiliar is not diametrically opposed to the familiar, since the familiar, because it is private and secret, contains in itself the suspicion of the strange. "*Unheimlich*," writes Freud, "is in some way or other a sub-species of *heimlich*" (131). In the same way, Borges points to the ambiguity—the disturbance, the similarity, the confusion—between the familiar face and its mask, between surprises and "portents as strange as surprises" (EC 38). In Borges, the familiar is always a possible source of the strange, just as the strange may turn out to be familiar. Of an unknown street, he writes:

> What is certain is that I felt it remotely near,
> like a memory which arrives exhausted
> only because it has come from the depths of the soul.
> Miracle of the glowing street,
> intimate and deeply stirring
> and only afterward
> I realized that that place was strange. (SP 7)

What would a man not do to organize and accentuate the games attributed to chance in order to reproduce those games, making their charge of strangeness manifest? Borges's question is answered by his own text.

Desire and Fear of Names:
Ineffective Simulacra

Referring to the inherent *unease* of Chesterton's fiction, Borges claims that "he defines the near by the far." The same phrase, in itself reversible, describes the estrangement typical of his own texts. I am not suggesting that the phrase describing Chesterton be applied to Borges's plots, nor to the elements in those plots that might generate the uncanny, like the tree in Chesterton or eyes in Hoffmann, even though such elements do play a part in Borges's fiction. It is more profitable, instead, to apply the statement about Chesterton to the *organization* of Borges's text, using the phrase "he defines the near by the far" to describe the grammar of a narrative at once distancing and deceptively familiar.

Any consideration of that grammar bringing together the familiar and the unfamiliar and ensuring their mutual contamination must take into account, as a constant, Borges's distrust of names. The distanced referent, the ambiguous signified, the ubiquitous signifier, do more than make manifest the precariousness of reader, author, character, and narrative situation, more than question the clearcut boundaries of the text containing them. In a broader sense, these unstable elements posit a sign that refuses to settle, reflecting an almost obsessive will to avoid names. For Borges, names—

names aspiring to account for a totality and not the fragments, or allusions, that his text offers—are clearly dangerous. For Borges, to name means to fix a segment of the text and proclaim it unique, disregarding the unsettling possibility that it may be a mere repetition, a simple tautology. For Borges, to name with such faith (or with such superstition) is to disregard William of Occam's economical principle, which he frequently cites: *Entia non sunt multiplicanda praeter necessitatem*, entities should not be multiplied in vain. In "A Yellow Rose," the Cratylian illusion that had kept Borges's Marino alive vanishes in one pathetic and terribly ironic moment, immediately preceding his death:

> Marino saw the rose, as Adam might have seen it in Paradise, and he thought that the rose was to be found in its own eternity and not in his words; and that we can mention or allude to a thing, but not express it; and that the tall, proud volumes casting a golden shadow in a corner were not—as his vanity had dreamed—a mirror of the world, but rather one thing more added to the world. (DR 38)

Entities should not be multiplied in vain. The signs left behind by Marino, the signs from which the yellow rose flees and whose useless, radiant materiality ("the tall, proud volumes casting a golden shadow in a corner") is stressed by Borges, are one more entity added to the world. Any sign, even when disguised, even when obliquely inscribed, as it is in Borges, always runs the risk of being *one more thing*, a superfluous accretion. Every sign accrues and multiplies.

As "The Postulation of Reality" posited a reality coincidental with literary verisimilitude, so the "world" invoked in this case is a textual world, an aggregate of letters. However, such a description is not always satifying for the simple reason that Borges's signs, while acknowledging that they are merely part of that written aggregate, at the same time, deceptively play at being more, or at being other, than that aggregate. It is as if the "verbal objects" called forth by a name could manifest themselves, like the verbal constructs in "Tlön, Uqbar, Orbis Tertius," as nonverbal objects, endowed with tangible materiality, in a realm beyond the signs in the text. As specious as it might be, such sophistry is integral to Borges's text, affecting its organization with the strength of real belief.

Borges suggests that Kafka and Hawthorne share not only an ethic ("Kafka's world is Judaism, and Hawthorne's, the wrath and punishments of the Old Testament" [OI 56]), but a rhetoric. Inverting the terms, one could say that in the work of Borges and that of some of his precursors, beyond a common rhetoric, there are shared elements of an ethic that sustain them in similar fashion. In this sense, Borges's references to the puritanical background of Hawthorne and Stevenson are no doubt something more than mere literary tributes. Indeed, for Borges, naming is a form of transgression, a heady temptation to create forbidden idols followed by the unease (or the repentance) caused by the production of simulacra, of perverted fabrications. Suffice it to recall the ironic *exempla* in "The Circular Ruins," and in "The Golem":

> The rabbi gazed fondly on his creature
> and with some terror. *How* (he asked himself)
> *could I have engendered this grievous son,*
> *and left off inaction, which is wisdom?*
>
> *Why did I decide to add to the infinite*
> *series one more symbol? Why, to the vain*
> *skein which unwinds in eternity,*
> *did I add another cause, effect, and woe?* (R 275)

For Borges, neither Stevenson nor Hawthorne (to whom he dedicated his best exercises in *sympathetic* criticism) ever "ceased to feel that the task of the writer was frivolous or, what is worse, even sinful" (OI 59). Borges recalls that the work of each author reenacts the "ancient dispute between ethics and aesthetics or, if you prefer, theology and aesthetics" (OI 59), attested in the Scriptures, in Platonic texts, and in Muslim doctrine, a dispute enriched by the speculations of idealism, ever present in Borges. A moment in Chuang Tzu's dream—" 'I dreamed that I was a butterfly flying through the air and that I knew nothing of Chuang Tzu' " (OI 184)—elicits the following commentary:

> There is no other reality for idealism than that of the mental processes; to add to the butterfly that is perceived an objective butterfly seems to be a vain duplication; to add a subject to the processes seems no less excessive. . . . The chronological determination of an event, of any event on earth, is alien and exterior to the event. (OI 184–85)

However often it comes up, the vanity of duplication never ceases to be for Borges a "difficulty (and not a mere illusion)" (OI 60).

It matters little whether Borges fully agrees or not with his puritanically minded forebears, whether or not he feels there is frivolity and sin in literary practice, as did Stevenson and Hawthorne. The fact is that, like them, with a quasireligious superstition, he fears the fixity of names and earnestly works against it while longing for it with equal earnestness. Statements comparing writing to sorcery are not uncommon in Borges, or rather, statements justifying certain sorceries, for no real reason other than his own sympathy. "Image is sorcery," he writes. "To transform a fire into a storm, as Milton did, is the feat of a sorcerer. To transmute the moon into a fish, a bubble, or a comet, as did Rossetti, erring before Lugones, is a lesser mischief" (I 28).

Borges does not go so far as to denounce characters for being puppets, artifices at the service of plot, as Stevenson did with zeal and a fair amount of candor. Nor does he link those artifices (as if atoning for them) to a moral intent as, in his view, did Hawthorne. On the contrary, he criticizes such an allegorical stance for producing "tiresome pleonasms" (OI 49). Yet both possibilities—denouncing artifice or transforming it into a moralizing fable—are not entirely alien to Borges; they are potential extremes between which he fluctuates. On one extreme is the Scotsman who, perhaps feeling guilty for having added "one more thing" to the world, renounced the construction of characters thus revitalizing romance as genre; on the other, the dour New Englander who, perhaps also feeling guilt and wishing to atone for it, reduced the ambiguous world of his dreams to didactic exercises and lost out as a narrator. Borges recalls how, in 1840, a homebound Hawthorne wrote in his diary as if to give himself substance: " 'If I had sooner made my escape into the world, I should have grown hard and rough, and been covered with earthly dust. . . . Indeed, we are but shadows . . .' " (OI 63). In its ambiguous nostalgia, the statement is not far removed from the resignation of "Borges and I" (L 246) or from this fragment from "Avatars of the Tortoise": " 'The greatest sorcerer (writes Novalis memorably) would be the one who bewitched himself to the point of taking his own phantasmagorias for autonomous apparitions. Would not this be true of ourselves?' I believe that it is" (OI 115).

Nostalgia for names, the tempting magic of names and, finally, the failure of names—simulacra the very moment they are uttered—are constants in Borges. It is no wonder that traitors abound in his stories: "Treason implies a fiction with a deceptive surface that shows itself and an underside that remains hidden and constitutes the treacherous core."[2] Aware of the failure of names, aware of the risk inherent in simulacra, Borges's text, nonetheless, perseveres. If the first tiger evoked in "The Other Tiger" is one more thing added and "not the deadly tiger," a second tiger will be named—even if "the act of naming it, of guessing / what is its nature and its circumstances / creates a fiction, not a living creature"—and then a third tiger. The simulacra produced in naming do not stop the search, however vain:

> Let us look for a third tiger. This one
> will be a form in my dream like all the others,
> a system and arrangement of human language,
> and not the flesh-and-bone tiger
> which, out of reach of all mythology,
> paces the earth. I know all this, but something
> drives me to this ancient and vague adventure,
> unreasonable, and still I keep on looking
> throughout the afternoon for the other tiger,
> the other tiger which is not in this poem. (R 282)

Distrust of names goes along with trust, in a form of give-and-take characteristic of Borges and already evident in his early *Inquisiciones*. In an essay in that book, "Después de las imágenes" [After Images], Borges envisions a writer who would surpass "the rogue and the sorcerer," a writer capable of naming without incurring in tautology, without just adding one more thing: "I speak of the demi-god, of the angel, whose works change the world. To bring realms into being, to hallucinate cities and domains of a total reality, is a heroic adventure" (I 28). The counterpart of that heroic, demiurgic adventure is contemplated, however, in the same essay. Naming may effect transfiguration, triumphant hallucination, but naming also reveals the tenuous foundation of such a presumption: "One must show an individual who walks into the mirror and remains in his illusory land (where there are symbols and colors, yet a still silence rules) and who feels the shame of being nothing more than a simulacrum, obliterated by nights, and only tolerated by the flickering light" (I 29).

Borges condemns the foolish attempt to add another illusion, another object, whose mere redundancy invalidates the world into which it is inserted. Differing from his precursors, the Greek philosophers he often resorts to, the Puritans with whom he sympathizes, Borges refrains from setting up possibilities for personal salvation or philosophical solace and does not rely on an ideal totality or on a founding Word for justification. For Borges, Platonic archetypes do not differ fundamentally from the Golem, so inept that even the rabbi's cat finds him unconvincing:

> [Archetypes] are not irresolvable: they are as confusing as the creatures of time. Made in the image of those creatures, they repeat the very same anomalies that they purport to explain. How could "Lionness," let us say, dispense with Fury or Redness, with "Maneness" or "Pawness"? There is no answer to that question, and there cannot be an answer: let us not expect from the term *Lionness* a quality superior to that of the same word without the suffix. (HE 21)

Borges's effort to deflect the explicit name, in order not to create *eidola*, in order not to be condemned to a single word that ultimately creates nothing except the *reflection* of itself, appears, as a challenge, throughout his work. On a narrative level, the most obvious expression of his avoidance of fixity is the subversion of expectation, of what the slothful reader deems inalterable. The characters in Borges's stories are doubles, are multiple, are finally anonymous. The plots of his fictions superimpose themselves on each other, deliberately altering previous stories, be they borrowed or his very own. They question their own originality, blur genealogy, and obliterate their point of departure. The quests undertaken by his characters (there is in Borges a faint echo of Bunyan) lead to emptiness, to elusive goals that fail to justify the pilgrim. The epiphanic moments in his stories are contaminated, as in "The Life of Tadeo Isidoro Cruz," or as in "The Zahir" and "The Aleph," deliberately debased by parody. Distrust of naming, of writing the word that would dangerously and unequivocally be fixed, is paralleled by the temptation of naming and perpetrating simulacra. Naming in Borges is an activity that is carried out obliquely, cautiously, also resignedly: it seeks not to create but to allude, fully conscious that allusion, although perhaps more humble, is also a way of naming.

To Name, To Falsify

The conjectural language proposed by Borges in "Tlön, Uqbar, Orbis Tertius" assiduously avoids the substantive: it corresponds to a world that for its inhabitants, "is not a concourse of objects in space; it is a heterogeneous series of independent acts" (L 8). Language, or rather, languages in Tlön (since Borges proposes two ways of avoiding the name for the two hemispheres of that planet) appear as a linguistic flow that instead of stopping on the substantive intermittently stops on its modifiers. In Tlön the mere act of naming, of classifying, "implies a falsification" (L 10). The same thing happens with numbers. The mathematicians of Tlön maintain "that the operation of counting modifies quantities and converts them from indefinite into definite sums" (L 12). In Tlön there are neither names nor numbers; there is no *moon* because an effort is made to have no *moon*. Like *l'absente de tous bouquets*, it goes unnamed, alluded to and convoked by a divergence—a "transposition," as Mallarmé called it—that eludes direct naming. In Tlön's southern hemisphere one does not say "The moon rose above the river" but (with Joycean zeal) "upward behind the onstreaming it mooned" (L 8). In Tlön's northern hemisphere, the substantive is avoided through the accumulation of adjectives: again there is neither moon, nor moons, but "round airy-light on dark" or "pale-orange-of-the-sky" (L 9).

Borges writes of these new combinations that they are "ideal objects, which are convoked and dissolved in a moment, according to poetic needs" (L 9). Both these ways of avoiding the substantive recall Marcus Flaminius Rufus's fruitless pedagogical experiment in "The Immortal." The Roman tribune conceives of a plan to teach the troglodyte "to recognize and perhaps to repeat a few words": "I gave him the name Argos and tried to teach it to him. I failed over and again" (L 112). In view of his futile efforts to impose a rudimentary nomenclature on the other, and in order to account for his failure, the tribune resorts to an extravagant fancy, no different from the one on which the languages of Tlön are based:

> I thought that Argos and I participated in different universes;
> I thought that our perceptions were the same, but that he com-
> bined them in another way and made other objects of them; I
> thought that perhaps there were no objects for him, only a ver-
> tiginous and continuous play of extremely brief impressions. I
> thought of a world without memory, without time; I considered
> the possibility of a language without nouns, a language of imper-
> sonal verbs or indeclinable epithets. (L 112)

These poetic objects, whose elusive and transitory character is emphasized by Borges, signal a provisional halt within the flow of language, within the "vertiginous and continuous play" of writing; it is the provisional break made by the speaker, the scribe. On a linguistic level, these pauses recall Hermann Lotze's argument, as quoted by Borges, to elude the "multiplication of chimeras." Lotze "concludes that there is one single object in the world: an infinite and absolute substance, comparable to the God of Spinoza. The transferable causes are reduced to immanent ones; events, to man-ifestations or modalities of the cosmic substance" (OI 112). In the same way, one might say that in Tlön there is a single object, an infinite, absolute linguistic substance, obeying the same purpose: it avoids the substantive—the emblem *par excellence* of the chimera, of the rigid, paralyzing simulacrum—in order to stop sporadically on manifestations ("upward behind the onstreaming it mooned") or on modalities ("round airy-light on dark") of that substance itself; manifestations lasting the time of their utterance or of their inscrip-tion. However, Borges himself is the first to point out the flaws of this utopian proposition based on the rejection of the one and only name: "The fact that no one believes in the reality of nouns para-doxically causes their number to be unending. The languages of Tlön's northern hemisphere contain all the nouns of the Indo-European languages—and many others as well" (L 9).

The fallacious identity proposed by coitus—"thus Venus de-ceives her lovers with simulacra," writes Borges quoting from Lu-cretius (HE 35)—the identity proposed by mirrors, by archetypes, by Cratylism, are vain attempts at reproduction. Plotinus's rejection of likeness is understood too late by the rabbi from Prague, the gray man in "The Circular Ruins," and the masked dyer of *A Universal History of Infamy*, all of them practitioners, in a way, of the "craft of the ungodly, the counterfeiter, and the shifty" (UHI 80). Reproduction is intolerable because, innocently, perhaps blindly, we expect from it an identical reflection. Instead, reproduction forces us to face the inadequacy of our attempt to call forth the identical, to confront the awkwardness of a "would-that-it-not-be" (TE 35). In "Death and the Compass," Red Scharlach comes to realize the illusory nature of his uniqueness and feels "that two eyes, two hands, two lungs are as monstrous as two faces" (L 84–85). In "The Immortal," Marcus Flaminius Rufus, confronting the monstrosity of parody, refuses to describe the City of the Immortals. It is not the harmonious whole he had dreamed in his mind, but "a kind of parody or inversion" (L 113): "a chaos of heterogeneous words, the body of a tiger or a bull in which teeth, organs and heads monstrously pullulate in mutual conjunction and hatred can (perhaps) be approximate images" (L 111). The copy, the repetition—a tautology in the case of Scharlach, a contradiction in the case of the Immortals, who destroy the first city in order to build its exact reverse—is, in both cases, monstrous and intolerable.

Equally intolerable, unavoidable, and monstrous is the reproduction effected by the author of any text. The narrator in "The Library of Babel" recalls that: "To speak is to fall into tautology. This wordy and useless epistle already exists in one of the thirty volumes of the five shelves of one of the innumerable hexagons—and its refutation as well" (L 57). Every text fatally *reproduces* a previous one, through reflection or inflection: it unsettles that previous text, that already inscribed sign, and at the same time it is unsettled by it. The *Quixote* of Menard and that of Cervantes—an extreme example of reproduction, also an exercise in literary modesty—set side by side are as disturbing as Red Scharlach's two eyes and two lungs: they are apparently redundant, yet necessary. Of the two people searching for a pencil in "Tlön, Uqbar, Orbis Tertius," the first perhaps offers the best example of verbal economy and mistrust of names: he finds the pencil and *says nothing* (L 13). We are not told if the second person, who finds a second pencil "closer to his expectations" (L 13) does say something; we are led to suspect that he might, thus adding one more thing to the world, incurring in the multiplication condemned by Borges.

Duplicates in "Tlön, Uqbar, Orbis Tertius" have peculiar characteristics: they "are, though awkward in form, somewhat longer" (L 13). In sum, these "secondary objects" replicate an unnamed "original" and at the same time, diverge from it. Additionally, they are endowed with the power to question and modify, a power that Borges usually associates with the practice of literature. The methodical elaboration of these secondary objects or *hrönir*, in Tlön, "has made possible the interrogation and even the modification of the past, which is now no less plastic and docile than the future" (L 14).

The description of Pierre Menard's reflections on chess may be applied to Borges's avoidance of names and his concomitant meditation on tautology, simulacra, and counterfeits. Contemplating the possibility of supressing a piece from the game of chess, Menard "proposes, recommends, discusses, and finally rejects this innovation" (L 37). In the same way, Borges seems to propose, recommend, discuss and finally reject the possibility of suppressing the name. The rejection of that possibility, leading to the resigned acceptance of the deficient name, manifests itself through divergence, a swerve neither greater nor smaller than the one separating the illusory original name from its imperfect simulacrum.

Duplications in Tlön differ from their "originals": they are more awkward and at the same time longer. Menard's *Quixote*, perhaps not awkward, is shorter: it consists of fragments literally identical to those by Cervantes. This lack of perfect coincidence (a divergence, one might say, in order to avoid tautology) is not simply a consequence of the *unfinished* nature of Menard's text. Rather, it is prompted by the same conditions governing the appearance of the *hrönir* in Tlön: *distraction* and *forgetfulness*. Pierre Menard, whose literary superstitions prevent him both from imagining the world without *Le Bateau ivre* or *The Rhyme of the Ancient Mariner* and from attempting to duplicate those texts, literally reproduces part of the *Quixote* in twentieth-century Nîmes. He can only do this because he believes that: "The *Quixote* is a contingent book; the *Quixote* is unnecessary. I can premeditate writing it, I can write it, without falling into a tautology. . . . My general recollection of the *Quixote*, simplified by forgetfulness and indifference, can well equal the imprecise and prior image of a book not yet written" (L 41).

Pascal, as imagined by Borges, must have avoided tautology in a similar way. Distracted, forgetful of a previous text, he worked out his conception of the universe: "It is an infinite sphere, the center of which is everywhere, the circumference nowhere" (OI 9). Less than a century before, Giordano Bruno, as Borges reminds us, had asserted that "the universe is all center, or that the center of the universe is everywhere and the circumference nowhere" (OI 8). And, centuries later, one of Borges's characters, describing the Library, or "the universe (which others call the Library)," again takes up the same dictum: *"The Library is a sphere whose exact center is any one of its hexagons and whose circumference is inaccessible"* (L 52). For Giordano Bruno, the exultant conception of the universe meant liberation; for Pascal, who writes the same words, as Menard writes those of Cervantes, the conception is frightening; for the narrator in "The Library of Babel," who repeats those words in turn, it is the point of departure of his lucid perplexity. Ultimately, neither Pascal, nor Menard, nor Borges's narrator, nor Borges himself, incur in reductive repetition: "they do not attempt to restore the difficult past—working with it, they digress from it" (D 9).

Considering the tautological nature of language, the narrator in "The Library of Babel" states that "an *n* number of possible languages use the same vocabulary; in some of them, the symbol *library* allows the correct definition *a ubiquitous and lasting system of hexagonal galleries*, but [in others] *library* is *bread* or *pyramid* or anything else, and the eight words which define it have another value" (L 57–58). Without going to the extremes suggested by this statement, one can say that the words defining the universe for Pascal, words identical to those of Giordano Bruno, have, in Pascal's code, a value *other* than the one they have in that of his precursor; and that the words of the narrator in "The Library of Babel" in turn have a value *other* than the one they have in the previous two codes: finally, that the words in Menard's *Quixote*, although they coincide exactly with the signs composing the words of Cervantes, are *other words*.

Borges delights in pointing out the transformations of a word repeated and yet different, the many ways in which a term, or a series of terms, considered fixed and final, may drift. In "The Lottery in Babylon," when the Company faces its critics: "with its usual discretion, [it] did not answer directly. It preferred to scrawl, in the ruins of a mask factory, a brief statement which is now part of the sacred scriptures" (L 33). The reverse of that derivation, in which a scribble becomes a canonical text, is, as the narrator in "Pierre Menard" points out, just as viable:

There is no exercise of the intellect which is not, in the final analysis, useless. A philosophical doctrine begins as a plausible description of the universe; with the passage of the years it becomes a mere chapter—if not a paragraph or a name—in the history of philosophy. In literature, this eventual caducity is even more notorious. (L 43)

The redundancy of names, the tautological nature of language, the illusion of simulacra both threatening and tempting, are saved by the intertextual *derivation* that Borges defends and puts into practice in his texts. In Tlön's conjectural *Ursprache*, the explicit mention of the word *moon* is not different from the unsettling modifiers that replace it and work against its rigidity: the moment they are uttered, both *moon* and the apparently mobile *round airy-light on dark* convey a falsification. But while *moon* falsifies without imagination, so to speak, its metonymic substitute, as it drifts, is capable of conversion.

In "A Vindication of Basilides the False," Borges details a cosmogony based on duplication and reflection, the work of "seven subordinate divinities," emanating from an immutable, nameless God, who, like the Rabbi of Prague, condescended to action and founded a series of hierarchical derivations. Borges concedes the apparent vanity of such multiplication; and yet, because it is *something more* than mere redundancy, he defends it:

[T]o scoff at the vain multiplication of the nominal angels and the reflected symmetrical heavens of that cosmogony is not at all difficult. The restrictive principle of Occam (*Entia non sunt multiplicanda praeter necessitatem*) could be applied to it, destroying it. As for me, I believe such rigor to be anachronistic or useless. The good conversion of those heavy, wavering symbols is what counts. (R 26)

The good *conversion* of those *wavering* symbols, just as the *diverse* intonation of a few *metaphors* (OI 9), is what counts for Borges. The practice of literature is nothing if not the result of the conversion and diverse intonation of the same word. Efficiently, dynamically, Borges's text proposes and at the same time effects that "good conversion," that "diverse intonation" of a word asking nothing more than to be unsettled, in order to fully reveal its unstable charge. Borges recalls that theologians "assert that the conservation of this world is a perpetual creation and that the verbs *to conserve* and *to create*, so antithetic down here, are synonymous in Heaven" (HE 33). In the same way, his text conserves and creates, through an elusive word, forever convertible.

Diversion, Conversion, Metaphor

Divergence, a divergence capable of conversion, is a constant in Borges's text. At first look, this attraction for divergence seems not too far removed from the recasting of metaphor proposed by avant-garde poetics. Borges himself recalls what was for the *ultraístas* an article of faith *par excellence*: "[M]etaphor excited us because of its precision, because of its algebraic way of correlating distant things" (I 97). However, the correlation of distant things carried out in Borges gradually abandons this simplistic, ultimately common-place conception of metaphor in order to give metaphor a different value.

In "The Kenningar" Borges defends the effectiveness of Icelandic tropes, an effectiveness he attributes to the heterogeneous contacts between the terms composing them and to the pleasurable wonder they generate. "They give an almost organic satisfaction," he writes. "What they mean to transmit makes no difference; what they suggest is nil. They do not beckon us to dream, nor do they provoke images or passions; they are not a point of departure; they are an end in themselves" (HE 46). Borges takes pleasure in pointing out the distance between name and trope. He recalls that "moon of the pirates is not the definition necessarily required by the shield" (HE 46), but that the reduction of the gap between "moon of the pirates" and "shield" would imply a "complete loss." He appreciates the somewhat monstrous "scapula's leg" to refer to a human arm because the kenning inscribes the fundamental and unexpected oddness of the human arm more efficiently than the substantive it replaces. But the Borges who takes note of such wonders has stopped sharing (if he ever truly did share) the pious belief of many of his contemporaries in the omnipotent virtues of avant-garde metaphor. When he discusses kennings he does so as an observer, keeping his distance: "the dead *ultraísta*, whose ghost still haunts me, enjoys these games" (HE 66). Beyond mere wonder, beyond the satisfaction suggested by these combinations, Borges divines an "awkward truth" (HE 44): that kennings were predetermined divergences from a name, mere literary conventions, perhaps no different from the Homeric epithets that, Borges suggests, "were what prepositions are today: modest, obligatory sounds added by use to certain words and which do not admit any originality" (D 107).

However, the study of kennings is not merely an exercise in nostalgia. If Borges lingers on them with obvious delight, it is above all because he intuits, beyond their probable mechanical character, the potential in those signs for recharging meaning, the wonder and the effectiveness renewed with each reading. Similarly, he would like to recover "the harsh and work-wrought words" of Anglo-Saxon grammar:

> Symbols of other symbols, variants
> On the English or the German (their descendants),
> Yet at some point in time they were fresh images
> And a man used them to invoke the sea or a sword.
> Tomorrow they will come alive again;
> Tomorrow *fyr* will not become *fire* but rather
> Some vestige of a changeable tamed god
> Whom no one can confront without feeling an ancient fear. (SP 153)

In "Versions of Homer," Borges points out that translations are nothing "but diverse perspectives on a moveable fact, a long series of tentative choices between omission and emphasis." To translate, here, is to read. "The need to change languages is not essential," adds Borges. "This deliberate play of our attention is not impossible within the same literature" (D 105). From his tentative reading of Homer, Borges concludes that the epithets were perhaps mechanical; yet, as with kennings, he reclaims them with an observation that is also applicable to the Icelandic tropes. For the modern reader, "they are expressions which recur, movingly so, out of turn" (D 107). (They are out of turn or, one might say, out of text, like the couplet from Quevedo that Borges nearly transforms into a kenning by isolating it and thus underlining its unexpected power: "His Grave the Fields of Flanders are / His Epitaph the bloody Moon" [HE 46].)

"The Kenningar" confirms Borges's unquestionable attraction

for what is out of turn, out of text, for *non-sense*. While Borges uses the latter term pejoratively, to speak of Gracián, ultimately the error he criticizes in Gracián is not so much his absurd use of surprising, figurative divergence as it is Gracián's awkward practice of explaining away the distance between the astonishing terms of his metaphors. Gracián errs in "the apposition of each name to its atrocious metaphor, in the impossible vindication of his non-sense" (HE 48). Good divergence, instead, "estranges us from the world" (HE 65), like the captive mermaid evoked by Borges. Gracián's useless vindication is not unlike the medieval chronicler's efforts to explain and classify that unfamiliar mermaid in an effort to domesticate her: "[H]e reasoned that she was not a fish because she knew how to spin, and that she was not a woman because she could live in the water" (D 85).

"Intelligence is economical and orderly," writes Borges, "and it considers miracles a bad habit. To accept those miracles would be to invalidate itself" (IA 103). If in the Borges who writes "The Kenningar" there remain traces of an original bewilderment before the miraculous, this bewilderment never yields, all along his work, to domestication or to the reductive ordering of what is, and must remain, strange. Borges entertains himself with the study of strangeness, of the diverse degrees of strangeness in an isolated metaphor. In addition, he entertains himself by imagining to what extent the strange character of a metaphor is marked by the reception of the reader, who chooses whether or not to recognize the strange, who *projects* estrangement in his or her own reading. For example, Borges considers an isolated metaphor: "With ferocious jaws, the fire devours the countryside." In the work of a contemporary *ultra-ísta* writer, he tells us, the metaphor "swayed by 'devouring fire,' becomes a cliché, equals zero . . ." (IA 105). Removed from this first possible context, an avant-garde that institutionalizes the element of surprise, the liberated metaphor increases its power to amaze, fostered by the reader's suppositions:

> Let us suppose that it is presented to me as coming from a Chinese or a Siamese poet. I will think: Everything becomes a dragon for the Chinese, and I will imagine a fire clear as a feast with flames writhing, and I will like it. . . . Let us suppose that I learn that the author of this representation is Aeschylus and that it was spoken by Prometheus (which is the case) and that the

imprisoned titan, tied to a rocky peak by Strength and Violence, harsh ministers, said it to the Ocean, a venerable old man who came to witness his misfortune in a winged chariot. Then the statement would seem to me good and even perfect, given the extravagant nature of the speakers and the distance (by now poetic) of its origin. I will do as the reader, who no doubt has suspended his judgment until he has clearly ascertained whose was the phrase. (IA 105–6)

Whose was the phrase, or what was its context: Almost didactically, Borges's entire work takes the reader from an inevitable surprise before an isolated poetical artifice, amazing in its solitude (an *ultraísta* image, a kenning, a fragmentary quote, the animals that "have just broken the vase" in the Chinese encyclopedia), to a more complex amazement provoked by the inclusion of these artifices in a linguistic continuum (the animals that have just broken the vase alongside the ones who appear to be flies from afar), to the amazement ultimately prompted by the arbitrary concatenation of any writing. The uncanny in Borges's text does not reside in the isolation of the strange, which might be easily classified, but in the strangeness of non-sense incorporated into his text, leveled by its grammar: diverse elements affect that non-sense, yet none obliterate it.

In "The Penultimate Version of Reality," Borges considers that "a wisdom based not on thought, but on mere classificatory convenience" (D 39) is suspect. His text carefully avoids such a convenience. Not only does it not classify: paraphrasing Marcel Schwob, one should say that it *declassifies*.[3]

6

Pleasure and Perplexity

"You may look in front of you, and on both sides, if you like," said
the Sheep; "but you can't look *all* round you—unless you've got
eyes at the back of your head."

Lewis Carroll, Through the Looking Glass

"The Diluter gives us first a few notes of some well-known Air,
then a dozen bars of his own, then a few more notes of the Air,
and so on alternately: thus saving the listener, if not from all risk
of recognising the melody at all, at least from the too-exciting
transports which it might produce in a more concentrated form."

Lewis Carroll, Phantasmagoria

The Repertory:
Selection, Disarticulation, Rescue

Borges's description of the ideal universe of Plotinus—"a select
repertory that does not tolerate repetition or redundancy" (HE
16)—is applicable to his own work. Yet the organization of Borges's
own "select repertory," that is, the basis for its syntax, not only
avoids redundancy and repetition but questions the very sequence
of words, a sequence that only the reader's laziness or superstition considers inevitable: "I have noticed that in general a reader
acquiesces to a story's rigorous, dialectical, sequential unfolding
merely because of an indolent inability to question the proofs
adduced by the writer and because of a vague confidence in his
honesty" (I 84).

To inscribe itself obliquely in a textual realm in which everything has been said, everything is repeated, and everything may be
transformed, Borges's text follows a process of selection based on

rupture and hiatus—based on that "monstrous" blank interstice underscored by Foucault in his preface to *The Order of Things*. In the problematic and deceitful Chinese encyclopedia imagined by Borges in "The Analytical Language of John Wilkins," "it is not the 'fabulous' animals that are impossible," writes Foucault, "since they are designated as such; what is impossible is the narrow distance separating them from (and juxtaposing them to) the stray dogs, or the animals that from a long way off look like flies."[1] That narrow distance guides Borges's haphazard, dissonant textual organization, even in apparently simple, seamless texts. The unnerving hiatus, the uncanny fissure, whether evident or concealed, underlie Borges's entire oeuvre, no different from the "chasm" in Hawthorne's *The Marble Faun*, whose description Borges significantly quotes in full:

> "I fancy," remarked Miriam, "that every person takes a peep into it in moments of gloom and despondency; that is to say, in his moments of deepest insight.
>
> "The chasm was merely one of the orifices of that pit of blackness that lies beneath us, everywhere. The firmest substance of human happiness is but a thin crust spread over it, with just reality enough to bear up the illusive stage-scenery amid which we tread. It needs no earthquake to open the chasm. A footstep, a little heavier than ordinary, will serve." (OI 62)

From the start, Borges's work calls attention to that precarious, thin layer superimposed over the chasm, a barely stable textual stratum sustaining a sign whose certainty is mere illusion. The precarious quality of that stratum, that Foucauldian "common place," is underscored by Borges's frequent references to disarticulation and decomposition. Calling personality "a Western superstition," Borges dwells on its disintegration: " 'Buddha Gautama is strictly equivalent to N.N.,' wrote Otto Franke; one might argue that Buddha wanted to be N.N."[2] Borges reflects on the decomposition of linear time, of literary history, of univocal, didactic thought, of an ordered, foreseeable narrative sequence, of round characters built up by the sheer accumulation of details. He dwells on disarticulation and decomposition as he writes about J. W. Dunne's shattering of time; about the deconstructive bent in the work of Herbert Quain; about Kafka creating his own precursors;

about the avatars of the tortoise; about the theologian John of Pannonia who disturbs the theologian Aurelian, just as Aurelian disturbs John of Pannonia; about Pierre Menard, who disturbs Cervantes; about Pedro Damián, who makes a ghost out of Pedro Damián, who in turns haunts Pedro Damián. Paraphrasing Parmenides, Borges never tires of affirming that the one is really many, and the one is also no one (OI 122).

Disarticulation—the fissure that Borges never loses sight of, that he does not allow his reader to forget—bears not only on the structure and the motifs of the story but on the inevitable succession of the signs themselves. In an early essay, "Indagación de la palabra" [Anatomy of the Word], Borges questions the possibility, proposed by Croce, that a single cognitive act is sufficient to grasp a text, and that reading consists of a single aesthetic revelation:

> Didn't Schopenhauer say that the form of our intellect is time, that narrowest of lines that only presents things to us one by one? The terrible thing about such narrowness is that the poems to which [Croce] reverentially alludes only achieve their unity in our meager memories, not in the successive efforts of whoever wrote them nor in the successive efforts of whoever reads them. (I said "terrible," because the heterogeneity of succession tears asunder not only an extended composition, but any single written page.) (IA 16)

Borges reflects more than once on that harrowing textual and linguistic dismemberment. In a later essay, he evokes Swift's horrible imagination in the third part of *Gulliver's Travels*, the men "incapable of talking with their brethren, because the course of time has modified language, and incapable of reading, because their memory fades from one line to the next" (OI 226). And Borges adds, "one may suspect that Swift imagined this horror because he feared it, or perhaps in order to magically exorcise it" (OI 226), which leads us to suspect that Borges refers to Swift's nightmare of verbal disintegration for similar reasons. Borges turns again to mutilation in the last paragraph of "The Immortal," as he quotes the last words of the man who was Homer, who was many men, who would soon be Nobody and also Everybody because he would soon be dead: " 'When the end draws near,' wrote Cartaphilus, 'there no longer remain any remembered images; only words remain.' Words, displaced and mutilated words, words of others, were the poor pittance left him by the hours and the centuries" (L 118).

Mutilation and displacement are the apex of a process of disarticulation that Borges practices and at the same time fears. Again, in his reading of Plotinus, he writes: " 'The objects of the soul are successive, now Socrates and then a horse,' I read in the fifth book of the *Aeneid*, 'always an isolated thing that is conceived and thousands that are lost; but Divine Intelligence encompasses all things' " (HE 14). For Plotinus, Divine Intelligence encompasses both the isolated things that remain as well as those that are lost. In doing so, it provides the series with a foundation that both justifies it and makes it intelligible; it imposes an order that domesticates the incongruous, shattered fragments, supressing the threat of hiatus. Instead, for Borges, fragments—mutilated words, isolated things, gaps—lack that reassuring foundation, or rather they themselves establish their own, hardly reassuring foundation, the "non-place of language," to borrow Foucault's phrase (xvii). The decomposition that drives Borges's text is ultimately to be found in that non-place of language, the shifting foundation of a sign that is itself shifting, that is susceptible to multiple readings. Like the poetic objects of Tlön, conjured up and dissolved in a moment, the elements that make up Borges's text fuse what is broken, displaced, heterogeneous, in the instant of writing, of reading: now Socrates and then a horse.

As if to underscore, by contrast, the arbitrary salvaging of disjointed pieces, Borges often dwells maliciously on notions of solidity, hardness, materiality, impenetrability. In "The Avatars of the Tortoise," he recalls that Bradley "denies all relations, . . . transforms all concepts into isolated, solidified objects. To refute him is to become contaminated with unreality" (L 206). This statement finds its narrative development in "Tlön, Uqbar, Orbis Tertius," where what is isolated and irreductible contaminates the verisimilitude posited at the beginning of the story, forces "reality" to yield, and installs itself in that "reality," disturbing it from within.

This insistence on the solid, the concrete, the material, parallels the process of disarticulation associated with Tlön, with its disorderly and contradictory multiplication of disjointed things. This is all the more remarkable since Tlön, unlike other utopias or counterutopias, is finally a non-place issuing from *language*. Tlön is a direct product of the *language and literature* of Uqbar; Uqbar, another non-place, comes out of a *text*, a blurry entry in the supplemental pages of an anomalous volume of the *Anglo-American Cyclopaedia*, revealing "beneath its rigorous prose a fundamental vagueness" (L 4). One aspect stands out in the nebulous description of Uqbar: "The section on Language and Literature was brief. Only one trait is worthy of recollection: it noted that the literature of Uqbar was one of fantasy and that its epics and legends never referred to reality, but to the two imaginary regions of Mlejnas and Tlön . . ." (L 5).

The story follows the description of Tlön, *one* of those two imaginary regions, extracted from a literature whose referents are in turn those very regions. Mlejnas is discarded, no longer functional in the text by the time a second *volume* appears in the story, volume eleven of *A First Encyclopaedia of Tlön*, as anomalous as the one from the *Anglo-American Cyclopaedia*. As the description of Tlön, based on this "vast, methodical fragment," becomes more foggy and perplexing, as Borges insists on disarticulating and displacing a literary projection that has become an independent entity, "hard" objects begin to appear in the world of Tlön: isolated copper coins, a concrete pencil, a gold mask, an archaic sword, clay urns, the mutilated torso of a king, and finally, projected into "our" world, a compass and a cone. The solid metal compass whose vibrations succeed in upsetting the "delicate, immobile objects" (L 16) that lie near it and the oppressively heavy small metal cone found by the narrator after a night of confusion are the most obviously dissonant objects, since they no longer intrude in Tlön but in the very world of the narrator.

Borges attributes both to Icelandic tropes and to the poems of Quevedo a hardness and a splendid isolation similar to those of verbal artifices in Tlön. He describes kennings as "verbal objects, pure and independent like a mirror or a silver ring" (HE 70). Using a virtually identical phrase, he calls Quevedo's sonnets "verbal objects, pure and independent like a sword or a silver ring" (OI 42). The terms of these comparisons are significant beyond their obvious mythological connotations: the mirror that reflects, the ring implying circularity, the sword that cuts, are all objects less independent than they appear at first glance. "Isolated, solidified objects," they suggest, at the same time, mobility and posit a relation. They circularly repeat; they reflect and refract; they cut and open. They take part in the give-and-take characteristic of Borges, like the inconstant mirror defining Borges's "Ars poetica":

> It is also like the river with no end
> That flows and remains and is the mirror of one same
> Inconstant Heraclitus, who is the same
> And is another, like the river with no end. (SP 159)

The Pleasure of Interpolation

"My account will be faithful: may Allah deliver me from the temptation of adding any circumstantial details or of weighing down the tale's Oriental character with interpolations from Kipling" (A 129), says the narrator of "The Man on the Threshold." It goes without saying that the tale he reconstructs neglects neither circumstantial details nor interpolation. The parodic invocation at the beginning of the story refers to two devices frequently used by Borges, perhaps the ones that give him, both as writer and reader, the most pleasure.

In Borges, oblique naming through refraction, disarticulation, or fragmentation implies the subversion of an expected order through *replacement,* while interpolation implies subversion through *addition.* Borges's delight in interpolation may well reside in that addition, just as it resides in the nature of the "world" where such an addition is effected. To name presupposes the risk of adding "one more thing"; to name is to add to the series. On the contrary, to interpolate satisfies the temptation to add without incurring the risk of creating redundant simulacra. To interpolate is to add to the series for the purpose of interrupting it, of modifying (perhaps canceling altogether) the elements that precede and that follow the interpolation. To interpolate is not to name: it is rather to work against fixity, to open a gap in a foreseeable series, *to delay.*

In the essay on "The Translators of the *Thousand and One Nights,*" Borges takes pleasure in the flaws of Edward Lane's version, which he considers the product of distraction: "Sometimes his lack of sensibility actually comes to his aid for it leads him to interpolate very simple words in a stately paragraph, with unwittingly good results" (HE 106). The "cooperation of heterogenous words" that Borges notices in Lane is not fundamentally different from the cooperation, or the counterpoint, between heterogenous sequences in other texts discussed by Borges or in his own. In Borges's Babylon, for example, it is believed "that the lottery is an interpolation of chance in the order of the world and that to accept errors is not to contradict chance: it is to corroborate it" (L 33).

Both in "The Perpetual Race of Achilles and the Tortoise" and in "Avatars of the Tortoise," Borges reflects on Lewis Carroll's reconstruction of Zeno's paradox. He does not consider it the most elegant version, nor the most faithful to Zeno—such distinction belongs, according to Borges, to William James. But Lewis Carroll's version is the one that contains the most interpolations, the most uncontrollable gaps, and the most humor. To begin with, Carroll interpolates a possibility that immediately invalidates the series. Carroll's version includes a quiet conversation between "the two athletes" at the *end* of the endless race (L 206). Their conversation, an exercise in interpolations, is rather a pseudo-logical debate. The tireless tortoise insists on provoking Achilles, forcing him to interpolate, first with indignation, then with resignation, an infinite hypothetical proposition, or an infinite series of hypothetical propositions, between the second premise of the syllogism and its conclusion. If a and b are valid, z is valid; if a, b, c, and d are valid, etc. Borges points out that Lewis Carroll "observes that the Greek's paradox involves an infinite series of distances which diminish, whereas in his, the distances grow" (L 207). And so they do, thanks to Achilles's docile reasoning and to the Tortoise's passion for asymptote, so to speak. Carroll's version, a humorous *trompe-raison*, is based on the pure pleasure of interpolation, not on the conclusion of a race that inexplicably has ended, nor in the culmination of clear, syllogistic reasoning, but on the pleasure of delaying closure and introducing gaps in an apparently coherent series of words.

As fixed and limited as they seem, the rules of the circuitous dialogue between Achilles and the Tortoise are not so different from the erratic progress of other series quoted or put into practice elsewhere in Borges. The dialogue's greatest charm resides in the unruly interpolations of the wise Tortoise, whose main virtue, like Croce's, seems to be "to cut short a discussion, not to resolve it" (R 30). The interpolations made by Achilles, encouraged by the

Tortoise, follow a foreseeable pattern, but with the incorporation of new hypothetical propositions, they distance themselves vertiginously from the premises on which the series was founded and from the conclusion suggested by those premises, so that the moment will come when infinite interpolations will erase the general framework that initially contained them. Like "the Hydra's adventitious heads that seem more concrete than its body" (HE 133), the adventitious propositions will then be no different from the broken, displaced words of the Immortal, from the words corroded by time and oblivion that Swift's characters cannot make coherent. Words, reasonings, signs whose meanings and referents become increasingly tenuous, all have lost the fragile structure that seemed to assure their coherence.

"The truth is that succession is an intolerable misery, and magnanimous appetites desire all the minutes of time and all the varieties of space" (HE 35), writes Borges. One might add that Borges's appetite also covets the fissures in that miserable succession and that it wastes no opportunity to dwell on those fissures in order to question the validity of the series. Borges reflects on Aquinas's *regressus in infinitum* as proof of the existence of God (OI 112). Yet he seems to prefer the hypotheses of those who, also working with succession and causality, upset them through interpolation. In "The Creation and P. H. Gosse," Borges recalls that John Stuart Mill reasoned that "the state of the universe at any instant is a consequence of its state at the previous instant and that for an infinite intelligence the perfect knowledge of a *single instant* would make it possible to know the history of the universe, both past and future" (OI 23). Yet significantly, Borges adds:

> Mill does not exclude the possibility that a future exterior intervention may break the series. He asserts that state q will inevitably produce state r; state r, s; state s, t; but he concedes that before t a divine catastrophe—the *consummatio mundi*, say—may have annihilated the planet. The future is inexorable, precise, but it may not happen. God lies in wait in the intervals. (OI 23)

In the same essay, Borges summarizes Gosse's explanation of causality. Like Mill, Gosse proposes a temporal series, rigorously causal and infinite, but broken by a past act—Creation—rather than by Mill's "future act of God." According to Gosse:

> State *n* will inevitably produce state *v*, but before *v* the Universal Judgment may occur; state *n* presupposes state *c*, but state *c* has not occurred, because the world was created at *f* or *h*. The first instant of time coincides with the instant of the Creation, as St. Augustine says; that first instant tolerates not only an infinite future, but an infinite past. A past that is hypothetical, to be sure, but also precise and inevitable. (OI 24)

Both reasonings appeal to Borges because they are founded on causality, but it is evident that they appeal to him even more because each one proposes, in its own way, a system of cause and effect marked by a break that questions—just as the infinite syllogism of the asymptotic Tortoise questions Zeno's paradox—the mania for concatenation. Mill establishes an inevitable and precise future; Gosse (whose reasoning Borges admires for its "rather monstrous elegance") establishes a precise and fatal past. In both series, *God lies in wait in the intervals.*

In similar fashion, Borges lies in wait and interpolates in the intervals of literary succession, no different from philosophical concatenation. After all, both philosopy and literature are no more and no less than "a coordination of words" (OI 114). Small wonder that Borges considers *Dreamtigers* his most faithful book: "Of all the books I have delivered to the presses, none, I think, is as personal as the straggling collection mustered for this hodge-podge, precisely because it abounds in reflections and interpolations" (DR 93).

Borges's fictions as well as his essays commend the practice of interpolation. In "The Lottery in Babylon," "No book is published without some discrepancy in each one of the copies. Scribes take a secret oath to omit, to interpolate, to change" (L 34). I have already mentioned how in stories with doubles, say "Story of the Warrior and the Captive" or "The Theologians" or "The Life of Tadeo Isidoro Cruz (1829–1874)," stories where the apparent binary pattern of narration should lead from *a* to *b*, an unforeseen third character is always interpolated to break the facile unfolding of the narrative. The same may be said of unforeseen texts. In "Theme of the Traitor and the Hero," the interpolation of quotations from Shakespeare in the string of moments that make up Kilpatrick's life does not add one more thing to the sequence of that life but radically alters it. A fragment from Schopenhauer, interpolated in a series of interpretations of Keats's "Ode to a Nightingale" (never read by Schopenhauer), unravels the critical framework set up by Borges in his essay (OI 122). Inversely, in "Kafka and His Precursors," Borges interpolates the name of Kafka in a series of names of disparate writers, thus creating an order *sui generis* that subverts the concatenation of cause and effect. In that series, *a* does not fatally produce *b*, nor *b*, *c*; on the contrary, the insertion of *k* modifies and reorganizes, giving the enumeration the deceptive appearance of a series: "If I am not mistaken, the heterogeneous pieces I have enumerated resemble Kafka; if I am not mistaken, not all of them resemble each other. This second fact is the more significant. In each of these texts we find Kafka's idiosyncrasy to a greater or lesser degree, but if Kafka had never written a line, we would not perceive this quality; in other words, it would not exist" (L 201).

The postscript to "The Immortal" ironically sums up the interpolations practiced in the story. An apocryphal commentator of Joseph Cartaphilus's story denounces, "in the first chapter, brief interpolations from Pliny (*Historia Naturalis*, V, 8); in the second, from Thomas De Quincey (*Writings*, III, 439); in the third, from an epistle to Descartes to the ambassador Pierre Chanut; in the fourth, from Bernard Shaw (*Back to Methuselah*, V). [The reader] infers from these intrusions or thefts that the whole document is apocryphal" (L 118).

"In my opinion," Borges adds with mock seriousness, "such a conclusion is inadmissible" (L 118). As is often the case with Borges's erudite references, the list of interpolations quoted in the postscript to "The Immortal" allows for the open, shameless exposition of the device that governs his unsettling patchwork.

Like any literary device that Borges finds attractive, interpolation is not exempt from danger. The danger, here, is not in naming but in *unnaming*, that is, in infinite ramification. The dialogue between Achilles and the Tortoise remains forever unfinished, as unfinished as the *Thousand and One Nights*, thanks to the interpolation of night DCII, whose story "embraces all the other stories as well as—monstrously—itself" (OI 45). "The curious danger" of this limitless interpolation is that it erases limits as it shifts positions foreseen by the text and by the reader: "those inversions suggest that if the characters in a story can be readers or spectators, then we, their readers or spectators, can be fictitious" (OI 46). However, given the choice between a stable continuum devoid of intervals, with no possibility of interpolation, and an endless possibility to interpolate that might end up in a "truncated story . . . infinite and circular" (OI 45), Borges does not hesitate. Considering "The Duration of Hell," he establishes a significant hierarchy of the horrors Hell has to offer: "The attribute of eternity is horrible. The one of continuity—the fact that divine pursuit lacks intervals, that in Hell no one dreams—is even more so, albeit impossible to imagine" (D 99).

Selective Erudition

The horror of continuity, mitigated by the pleasure of interpolation, is particularly evident in Borges's quirky erudition. If Borges undercuts certainties in his stories, putting into effect a sort of narrative *trompe-l'oeil*, in his essays, through erudition, his *trompe-l'oeil*, as has already been pointed out, becomes *trompe-raison*, questioning canonized certainties and textual monumentalization.

The verification and systematization of Borges's erudite references—references that are accurate, borrowed, more or less unorthodox, or simply invented—are a worthless task. In one of the first French readings of Borges, Etiemble pointed out that Borges referred to the *Hung Lu Meng*, "but in such a way that one would have to be very clever to find out if he had indeed read it (at a time when few Western readers could so much as cite the exact titles of *two* Chinese novels)."[3] In fact it hardly matters whether Borges refers directly to works he has read or to commentators of those works. Suffice it to show how flippantly he deals with prestigious erudition and literary hierarchy: when speaking of Joyce's *Ulysses*, he refers his reader to "Stuart Gilbert's descriptive book or, in its absence, to the dizzying book itself" (R 38). In "Tlön, Uqbar, Orbis Tertius," he calmly accepts the possibility that references to an article in the *Anglo-American Cyclopaedia*, made by Bioy Casares during a discussion, are "a fiction devised by Bioy's modesty in order to justify a statement" (L 4). The reader is in turn forced to accept, with considerably less calm, that all the references in "Tlön, Uqbar, Orbis Tertius" are merely a fiction improvised by Borges's modesty, or mischief, in order to justify a text.

It would be a mistake to accept Borges's profuse system of

references and quotations with the respect and "incredulous stupor" that the author himself condemns. At the same time, it is equally pointless to systematically doubt all references and quotes. The irreverence and irony underlying Borges's erudition are not necessarily proof of its spurious nature. Borges makes no claim to authenticity; he goes beyond it, and even seems to invite the discovery of fraud, precisely because such a discovery in no way signals failure. With regard to erudition, notions of truth and falsehood are absolutely lacking in value. It is therefore vain to impose ethical criteria on an erudition that aspires to be literary, in the richest sense of the term.[4]

In one more effort to push Borges into known categories, Marcial Tamayo and Adolfo Ruiz Díaz attempt to describe his erudition. They start out with a general classification of all quotations as either "ornamental" or "argumentative." Ornamental quotations play on prestige: inevitably boastful, they create a significant pause in the text, calling attention to themselves. Useless in terms of referential "information," they are more like stylistic mannerisms. On the other hand, argumentative quotations, those whose purpose is to add to the reading by bolstering an argument, frequently rely on a ponderous critical and bibliographic system of notes and appendices. In this case, mere decoration disappears before a clearly utilitarian purpose.[5]

Once they have made that distinction, however, Tamayo and Ruiz Díaz are hard put to classify Borges's references within the binary system they themselves have devised. Forced to admit that references in Borges, although they may approach the argumentative type "because of their reasoning, discursive quality," cannot be satisfactorily classified in that category, they are also forced to admit that Borges's references cannot be classified in the second category either. After concluding the obvious, that indeed "to write, Borges already moves in a web of references," these scholars prudently decide that "it is a delicate subject and it is not wise, led by a desire for critical ingenuity, to overstep the boundaries of what may be proved" (19).

What is so obvious that it needs no proof is that Borges's text is, so to speak, an already quoted text. It is not a question of overstepping "the boundaries of what may be proved" because those boundaries have already been crossed (and thus incorporated) in a text that challenges, or remains indifferent to, any reductive attempt to decipher it. The difficulties inherent in any attempt to classify Borges's erudition according to traditional patterns seem to suggest that quotes, references, and allusions require a different interpretation. As a man of Western culture, Borges might have been content with argumentative references. As an inquisitor of that very same culture, he might have mimicked ornamental references. The fact that references and quotations are neither one nor the other, that they neither reinforce an argument nor do they "decorate" it, that they function in a state of permanent *dissatisfaction* and replicate that dissatisfaction in the reader, shows that they are driven by a different spirit.

Few quotations and references battle as much as Borges's against the linear development of the narrative. In general, whether it creates temporary distance or immediate expectancy, a quotation is an ally of the text. If it may for an instant disorient the reader, as soon as it is processed it has the opposite effect, that of confirming the reader's intuitions. The distance thus created is illusory, the break marked by the quotation no break at all, for its purpose is after all to reassure the reader by safely returning him or her to the textual drift preceding the quote. Borges's impertinent use of quotes and references is eloquent proof that reassuring the reader is the last thing on his mind. After all, no one knows one's reader better than the author. For example, Unamuno accumulates references that may appear unsettling but that ultimately do not disturb the text. The text and its quotations point in the same direction, the latter confirming the former, open and available to the reader's recognition. If Borges piles up quotes and references, he does so with a different purpose in mind. For what sort of recognition can be expected in the reading of a text that, for instance, cites in the same breath the names of Chesterton, Estanislao del Campo, von Stenberg, and James Joyce? (D 90–91). And if this example seems harmless to an Argentine reader, what about a text that combines the names of Nils Runeberg, Lars Peter Lanström, Axel Borelius, three of the Evangelists, Saint Paul, Erik Erfjord (a Danish Hebraist, we are told, either to enlighten or to bewilder us), Euclides da Cunha, Almafuerte, Borges's childhood friend Maurice Abramovicz, and Borges's own fictional character, Jaromir Hladik? (L 98). Different sections of these impressive enumerations will be recognized by different readers; the two or three names that any one of those readers recognizes will goad her or him into a useless venture, that is, the attempt to recognize and decode every single reference. The distance introduced by Borges's quotations is not the distance of prestige, but of suspicious unease. Defying recognition, these quotations nonetheless refuse to be mere games or private jokes. Thus the reader wavers between the temptation to enjoy them for their exoticism and the temptation to decipher, and thus domesticate, the origins of such erudition. Because such references come from the most unexpected sources, the reader feels (or thinks that he or she is expected to feel) that they are held together by a critical argument whose mystery is unfathomable. Part of the unease, and the pleasure, provoked by such a reading comes precisely from the oscillating, dizzying quality of those references, which on the one hand attract and trap the reader, as if he or she were one more quotation, while on the other hand, they reject the reader from a text that he or she will never be able to appropriate. In the same way that the woman, the saddle, and the bay horse stand between Bandeira and Otálora in "The Dead Man" (A 93–99), in the same way that "the intruder" comes between the two brothers in the story of the same name, erudition mediates between writer and reader. It is a shifting attribute: the effort to appropriate it is pointless since it will never belong to either one, or it will briefly belong to one only to become contaminated by the vain, fragmentary desire of the other. Like Juliana in "The Intruder," it "set[s] a wedge between them" (DB 67).

The disquiet brought upon the reader by Borges's ambiguous erudition, at once attractive and forbidding, increases when, in the system of references and quotations made up of recognizable and unrecognizable cultural allusions that the reader has come willynilly to accept, there appears a break of a different kind, what one might term a regional uncanny. For Borges's erudition is indeed about the active pleasure of interpolation and not only about tacit, unexpected contacts. Fragments of "reality" recur in Borges's texts, breaking into series of quotes and literary references with disquieting effect, disturbing all sense of limits, of personal immunity. Think, for example, of Adolfo Bioy Casares, Enrique Amorim, and Carlos Mastronardi, contemporaries and friends of Borges who appear in "Tlön, Uqbar, Orbis Tertius" both as quotable sources and as characters. The reader for whom these names are familiar, who may even know the men behind these names—that is, the reader who shares Borges's cultural context—is taken aback to see them thus "quoted" and, like the fictional Herbert Ashe, "suffering from unreality": they have been transformed into cultural references, leveled by erudition. But the reader who does not know these names (or these men) will read them on the same level as the names of Gunnar Erfjord or Silas Haslam, and will not be wrong in doing so. For that is how they will be read, after all, when no individual traces, no actual referents, remain; when, in a future reading, they become what they always were, signs in a text.

   This type of cultural allusion creates an unreality effect because it is recognized as being too immediate, too familiar. The mention of the name of Bioy Casares, for example, a close friend and collaborator of Borges, would seem to impose the weight of its referent on the mere sign, and that startles the reader. Yet Borges's interferences point to something more than the unease prompted by the contact between a "real," "living" Bioy Casares and a fictional Silas Haslam. The reverse operation is also startling, that is, the inclusion of signifying segments, devoid of an immediately recognizable referent, in Borges's text: "When the blood ran through his fingers, he fought with more courage than ever" (A 82–83), writes Borges in "The Life of Tadeo Isidoro Cruz." The statement, perhaps as insignificant to a contemporary reader as the mention of Bioy Casares to a reader unfamiliar with Argentine literature or to a future general reader, remotivates, word for word, a statement found in another, seldom read book. In *Pilgrim's Progress*, Bunyan writes, "and when the blood ran through my fingers, then I fought with most courage." Recognizing Bunyan's phrase in a new version of a gaucho poem is as startling as recognizing Bioy in a fantastic narrative.

   These two examples of literary disruption have an element of surprise in common, an astonished "how can *this* be here." In the first example, a familiar, "living" author is incorporated into a fiction both as a secondary character and a textual reference. In the second, a fragment from Bunyan, remote and possibly unfamiliar to the reader, is revived in order to enhance, significantly so, a detail in the story. The two examples are less important in themselves than as emblems of the function of erudition in the work of Borges. For in future readings, when Bioy will be as anonymous as Silas Haslam, when Borges may be as anonymous as Bunyan, no doubt the two examples cited will not only not startle, they will go unnoticed. This does not mean that the system of erudite quotation and cultural allusion, as a whole, will lose its potential to disturb but that that potential will be displaced: new sympathies, new differences, new interstices will appear in the text. The tantalizing distance of Borges's erudition will always retain its lure, like the sirens evoked by Blanchot, who sang "in a way that was not satisfying, that only implied in which direction lay the true sources of the song, the true happiness of the song."[6] After all, what is the function of this vast system of erudition, to which Borges resorts to speak of *anything whatsoever* (a levity that immediately discredits any "serious" notion of erudition), but to mark a distance with respect to a text that the reader longs to domesticate and that permanently thwarts him? Erudition in Borges does not differ greatly from the "gradual deceptions" that govern the game of masks in his early fiction. It is a sign, as evident as it is faithful, of a vision of literature that rejects the fixed name, the perishable perfect page, proposing new directions as it questions the predictability of the system.

Exaggeration and caricature are notorious characteristics of Borges's erudition, characteristics that shamelessly mock literary smugness. To quote Chesterton and Joyce, one after the other, appears to confirm the centrality of Western culture. But to add to these names those of Estanislao del Campo and Almafuerte, or those of Erik Erfjord, and his elusive relative Gunnar, is not, as a naive Westerner might think, an enriching gesture, a call to a fecund cosmopolitanism on a universal scale. It is simply to laugh at (with) the reader. The references to Chesterton and Joyce are neither reinforced nor enhanced by the addition of an Argentine writer, or a Danish Hebraist, or the author of a German philosophical dictionary, or eventually, of some Argentine *femme du monde* whom Borges endows with the gift of words. Rather, their prestige—that of Chesterton, of Joyce, of Western culture—is, if not destroyed, at least seriously compromised by the added names. To give recognizable references is to remain within the traditional limits of literary decorum; it is to intensify an idea that pertains both to an individual and, reassuringly, to literary tradition. A recognizable quote is like a convocation that, for a moment, reunites the author of the text, the one who cites it, and the reader, under the comforting sign of Culture. But to quote irreverently as Borges does, vigorously shaking the problematic edifice of erudition, combining in wise disorder well known references and quotations with unknown or invented ones, does more than question the limits of that culture: it suppresses them, not through outright condemnation but through exaggeration and parody.

Borges's distancing quotations recall Brecht's alienation effects. Borges's erudition is every bit as disjointed as the scattered bits of scenery that attract Brecht to the work of Breughel the Elder, the Alpine peaks set in Flemish landscapes, the "old Asiatic costumes" next to modern dress, so that "the one denounces the other and sets off its oddness. . . . Even though Breughel manages to balance his contrasts he never merges them into one another."[7] Like Breughel, Borges does not merge contrasts into one another; yet, unlike Breughel, he does not really attempt to balance them. Borges stresses artifice through overt quotation. Like Brecht's Chinese actor, who "limits himself from the start to simply quoting the character,"[8] Borges's text limits itself from the start to quoting literature.

Brechtian distance, however, depends on a frank, almost didactic revelation, so that spectators know that they are "in the theatre." Borges, vying for a similar result through quotation so as to let readers know that they are "in literature," prefers provisional, indecisive allusion. For example, Estanislao del Campo's dramatic poem, *Fausto*, is hardly effective in Borges's opinion because its exposure of theatrical convention is sudden, uncritical, and lacking in nuance; because "the contamination is produced at the very outset of the story by a single reference to stage scenery" (EC 103). "The unreality of the outskirts is more subtle" (EC 103), adds Borges, describing the "ambivalent material" out of which Evaristo Carriego, the poet of the outlying boroughs, creates his work. Borges works with the same ambivalent material, on the margin. His erudite references, pitting author and reader against each other in an illusory struggle, are but another version of the unfulfilling "song from the abyss," which, to quote Blanchot once more, "once heard . . . opened an abyss in every utterance and powerfully enticed whoever heard it to disappear into that abyss" (106). Borges's text invites us to a similar abyss, an abyss opened by each word, by each quote that is never quite assimilated, that permanently shows itself and its difference in every register of discourse; a word, a quote, always conscious of its double, its multiple, pull.

7

The Buried Foundation

A crest of foam in the wide plain of the sea *from time to time* catches
the light: these *times* too are the creation of chance.

Paul Valéry, *Mélanges*

In reality all chance follows a set direction, it is governed by the
voracity of meaning.

José Lezama Lima, *Saint-John Perse: historiador de las lluvias*

Heterogeneous Enumeration and Overcrowded Series

Borges rejected Gabriel Miró's description of Herodias in *Figuras de
la Pasión de Nuestro Señor* because "thirteen or fourteen terms make
up this chaotic series; the author invites us to view those *disjecta
membra* as a single coherent image. Such a mental operation is
impracticable. . . ."[1] Yet heterogeneous enumeration and *disjecta
membra*, while avoiding combination within a *single* coherent image, are not uncommon in Borges's work. "A History of Eternity,"
for example, underscores the multiple monstrosity of the Trinity, "a
deformity that only the horror of nightmare could bring forth" (HE
25). Anomalous combinations are again the subject of one of his
film reviews, in which he speaks against dubbing:

> The possibilities of the art of combination are not infinite, but
> they are apt to be frightening. The Greeks engendered the chi-
> mera, a monster with the head of a lion, the head of a dragon, and
> the head of a goat; the theologians of the second century, the
> Trinity, in which the Father, the Son, and the Holy Ghost are in-
> extricably linked; the Chinese zoologists engendered the *ti-yiang*,
> a bright red, supernatural bird equipped with six legs and four
> wings but with neither face nor eyes; the geometrists of the

nineteenth century, the hypercube, a four-dimensional figure that encloses an infinite number of cubes and is bounded by eight cubes and twenty-four squares. Hollywood has just enriched this frivolous teratological museum: by means of a perverse artifice they call dubbing, they offer monsters that combine the sublime features of Greta Garbo with the voice of Aldonza Lorenzo. How can we fail to proclaim our admiration for this distressing prodigy, for these ingenious audio-visual anomalies? (Cozarinsky, *Borges in and on Film*, 62)

Once again, Borges's text forces his reader to hesitate between fear (near repugnance, in this case) and attraction. In his *Manual de zoología fantástica* [Manual of Fantastic Zoology], Borges invents or describes combinations that are no less monstrous. He evokes a child's wonder on his first visit to the zoo: "when he first sees the senseless variety of the animal realm, the spectacle, instead of scaring or horrifying him, pleases him" (MZF 7). And he adds: "The reader of this manual will discover that the zoology created by human dreams is less varied than the zoology created by God" (MZF 8). The positive connotations of the monstrous are not unusual in Borges: he uses Pliny's definition, *monstrorum artifex*, to describe two of his favorite authors, Wilde (OI 79) and Chesterton (OI 83). However, the making of monsters becomes intolerable for the narrator of "The Immortal." The "vile City of the Immortals" frightens and sickens him, not only because it is a simulacrum or a parody but because it illustrates the horrible union of the mismatched: "a chaos of heterogenous words, the body of a tiger or a bull in which teeth, organs and heads monstrously pullulate in mutual conjunction and hatred can (perhaps) be approximate images" (L 111).

The chaotic conglomerate produced by this "mutual conjuction and hatred" may be repugnant, but the repugnance it elicits may be tempered, for example, by pathos. Such is the case of the Minotaur in "The House of Asterion": "Like children, he repeats a simple number to signify the many. . . . In fact, more than a monster, the Minotaur is a freak. . . . An ambiguous, odd creature, he is fatally condemned to solitude."[2] Repugnance also may be lessened by parodic exaggeration, as in the horrible, yet ludicrous text written by Aurelian in "The Theologians" in order to differ from John of Pannonia:

> He erected vast and almost inextricable periods encumbered
> with parentheses, in which negligence and solecism seemed
> forms of scorn. He made an instrument of cacophony. . . . Au-
> gustine had written that Jesus is the straight path that saves us
> from the circular labyrinth followed by the impious; these Au-
> relian, laboriously trivial, compared with Ixion, with the liver
> of Prometheus, with Sisyphus, with the king of Thebes who
> saw two suns, with stuttering, with parrots, with mirrors, with
> echoes, with mules working a water wheel and with two-horned
> syllogisms. (L 120)

Aurelian's series is relatively innocuous, even ridiculous, because, monstrous though it is, it has only one purpose, the denun-
ciation of impiety. Of more interest, in Borges, are the series in
which point of departure and goal disappear, series in which dis-
tinct elements are exposed, one after the other, and where there are
no points of contact.

In his enlightening essay on Stevenson, oddly effective when
applied to Borges, Leslie Stephen emphasizes Stevenson's antipa-
thy for the predictable, his "hatred of the commonplace formula."
Quoting Stevenson on the need to condense, Stephen writes:
"There is but one art, . . . the art to omit; or, as Pope puts it, perhaps
more accurately, 'the last and greatest art' is 'the art to blot.' "[3]
Borges's own blotting is not, however, a form of reticence or under-
statement; his deletion of links is so surprising that it is enough to
question the coherence of the series itself. In fact, the deletions may
become more important than the remaining terms. As in the case of
the hydra, one loses sight of the "original" body, that is, the visible
text, to concentrate on the adventitious, the mute gaps between the
terms. Borges's series give the reader pleasure, but it is an *unfounded*
pleasure. "Eternity is the style of desire," Borges writes, and adds
suggestively: "It is plausible that in the hint of the eternal, in the
"inmediata et lucida fruitio rerum infinitarum, may be the cause of the
special pleasure produced by enumerations" (HE 37). The style of
desire in Borges coincides and does not coincide with such fruition.
His enumerations seem to thrive both on the immediacy of infinite
things and on the pleasures of constant interruption. Borges's explicit series are paralleled by concurrent series of omissions, of gaps
as arbitrary as the terms appearing in the series.

Enumerations in Borges are based on the principle that "there is no classification of the universe that is not arbitrary and conjectural" (OI 104). In addition, enumerations prompt us to "suspect that there is no universe in the organic, unifying sense inherent in that ambitious word. If there is, we must still conjecture its purpose; we must conjecture the words, the definitions, the etymologies, the synonymies of God's secret dictionary" (OI 104). Applicable to the universe, this conjecture is also applicable to literary discourse, and, for that matter, to any discourse. Thus all enumerations are possible, haphazardly combined into arbitrary statements. A phrase in Proust aptly summarizes Borges's use of enumeration: "It is our noticing them that puts things in a room, our growing used to them that takes them away again and clears a space for us."[4]

In "Funes the Memorious," it is obvious that the character's "noticing," his unflagging attention, generates the story's overwhelming enumerations. Funes's attention is untouched by the force of habit, by dreams, or by oblivion—all distractions that might, as Proust puts it, "clear a space." Funes's attention is the *common ground* holding together disparate elements, allowing them to come together as a repulsive nightmare, bloated with details. "My mind, sir," Funes tells the narrator, "is like a garbage heap" (L 64). Habit allows us to suppress, to blot the singularity of an object, to generalize: "We, at one glance, can perceive three glasses on a table" (L 63). Free of our globalizing sweep, Funes's attention meticulously breaks down the perception into a fatally metonymic series, registering previous stages that we have obliterated; false previous stages, that is, because for Funes all things appear at the same level of perception. While "we, at one glance, can perceive three glasses," Funes, among other, infinite things, perceives the three glasses, but also the wine in those glasses and "all the leaves and tendrils and fruit that make up a grape vine" (L 63). Funes's attention, the equivalent of total recall, allows for extraordinary memories: "He knew by heart the forms of the southern clouds at dawn on the 30th of April, 1882." It also allows him to line up, in what might be described as a metonymic linkage of metaphors, images for him analogous and contiguous to those southern clouds, accumulating but never substituting each other: "He knew by heart the forms of the southern clouds . . . and could compare them in his memory with the mottled streaks on a book in Spanish binding he had only seen once and with the outlines of the foam raised by an oar in the Río Negro the night before the Quebrancho uprising" (L 63).

Funes's unswerving attention also allows him to isolate the smallest element in a series, to translate the whole into accumulated details and thus abolish it: "A circle drawn on a blackboard, a right triangle, a lozenge—all these are forms we can fully and intuitively grasp; Ireneo could do the same with the stormy mane of a pony, with a herd of cattle on a hill, with the changing fire and its innumerable ashes, with the many faces of a dead man throughout a long wake. I don't know how many stars he could see in the sky" (L 64). Ireneo Funes's implacably focused attention preserves a "useless catalog of all the images of his memory" (L 65) in which there is no gap that is not filled by that very attention. Predictably, the singularity of the individual enumerating the series is abolished. Attention turns him into "the solitary and lucid spectator of a multiform, instantaneous and almost intolerably precise world" (L 65), a world in which the "hapless Ireneo" exists only as one more trivial element in the catalog. Indeed, after the accident that endows him with total recall, Funes stops paying attention to himself: "Somewhat later he learned that he was paralyzed. The fact scarcely interested him. He reasoned (he felt) that his immobility was a small price to pay. Now his perception and his memory were infallible" (L 63).

Mundane prolixity overwhelms Funes, engulfing him. As the narrator points out, "It was very difficult for him to sleep. To sleep is to turn one's mind from the world" (L 66). During his sleepless nights, Funes dwells on images that are curiously evocative; a crevice, darkness, the current of a river, all metaphors suggesting escape from the rigid system created by his ever wakeful attention, images of flow and imprecision that might clear a space for him. However, even those attempts at liberation are blocked, returning the attentive cataloger to the overcrowded series in which he barely has a place. Yes, Funes imagines every *crevice* in the houses that surround him, but he also imagines, in the very same houses, every *molding*: the gap is replaced by its sharply defined, protruding negation. In the same way, he limits the image he has of darkness, denying all possibility of imprecision, replacing porousness by compactness: "Toward the east, along a stretch not yet *divided into blocks*, there were *new houses, unknown* to Funes. He imagined them to be black, *compact*, made of *homogeneous darkness*" (L 66; my emphasis).

There is no place for Funes in the compact multiplicity of houses produced by his permanent attention, his incessant cataloging. Nor is there room for him in the other images that come to him in his half-sleep as the opposite of his tenacious accumulation. The fluid image of a river, while opposing the compactness of Funes's catalog, also cancels out Funes: "He would also imagine himself at the bottom of the river, rocked and *annihilated* by the current" (L 66; my emphasis). The futility of Funes's cataloging leads to the refuse heap, to useless accumulation. For Funes the possibility of selecting, of condensing, of blotting, does not exist. It is no wonder that the narrator suspects that "he was not very capable of thought" (L 66).

Two projects take up Funes's voraciously attentive mind, two types of enumeration. The first, discussed above, is the catalog of all the images of his memory. The second is "an infinite vocabulary for the natural series of numbers" (L 65). While both are the result of a Proustian "noticing," Funes's attention functions differently in each one. On the one hand, his exhaustive catalog of memories is ruled by metonymic obssession. The development of the series, even when it consists of metaphors, is ruled by contiguity. "Incapable of ideas of a general, Platonic sort" (L 65), Funes enumerates the elements that make up his fragmented, instantaneous vision in an unceasing process of semantic predication. The southern clouds at dawn are followed by the streaks in a book and by the foam raised by an oar. The mane of a pony is followed by the manes of many ponies next to it; the dog seen at three fourteen (from the side) is followed by the dog seen at three fifteen (from the front). On the other hand, the infinite vocabulary for the series of numbers seems to correspond to a disturbance of that contiguity, making the gaps between the terms much more evident. In this case, Funes does not link his terms by association, at least, an association the reader understands; he operates, rather, by substitution, but by a substitution not based on metaphoric analogy but by apparent non sequitur:

> In place of seven thousand thirteen, he would say (for example) *Máximo Pérez*; in place of seven thousand fourteen, *The Railroad*; other numbers were *Luis Melián Lafinur, Olimar, sulphur, the reins, the whale, the gas, the cauldron, Napoleon, Agustín de Vedia.* Instead of five hundred, he would say *nine.* Each word had a particular sign, a kind of mark; the last in the series were very complicated. . . . (L 64)

The two systems offer obvious differences beyond the organizing criteria that guide them. The blotting that Funes appears not to put into practice in the first, bloated series would seem to be at work in the noticeable gaps in the second. To go from *the dog at three fourteen* to *the dog at three fifteen* is not to go from *the cauldron* to *Napoleon*. However, the two sets of enumerations are both equally justified in Funes's mind, where there are no lapses, no hiatus. The narrator remarks on Funes's numbering system: "I tried to explain to him that this rhapsody of incoherent terms was precisely the opposite of a system of numbers. I told him that saying 365 meant saying three hundreds, six tens, five ones, an analysis which is not found in the 'numbers' *The Negro Timoteo* or *meat blanket*. Funes did not understand me or refused to understand me" (L 64–65). However, the two systems, though organized diversely, appear equally crowded and equally unpredictable to the reader. The narrator calls them "senseless, yet betray[ing] a certain stammering grandeur" (L 65). Sustained by Funes's attention, they finally *make sense* only to him. Indeed, all that holds them together—thus the narrator's inability to *reproduce* them—is Funes himself.

In "Funes the Memorious" and in "The Aleph" the scene of enumeration is prepared in almost identical terms. As soon as enumeration appears in the text, narrative verisimilitude, posited in both stories through abundant reference to local, nostalgic, even autobiographical trivia (evocations of nineteenth-century Uruguay, of twentieth-century petty-bourgeois Buenos Aires), ceases to play a role. The interruption signaled by enumeration, the cut that unsettles the narrative, mocks that elementary verisimilitude, calling attention only to itself. "I now arrive at the most difficult point in my story" (L 63), writes the narrator of "Funes the Memorious"; "I arrive now at the ineffable core of my story. And here begins my despair as a writer" (A 26), writes the narrator of "The Aleph." It is no wonder that the chronicler of "The Aleph" refers to his "despair as a writer." The series in "Funes" and in "The Aleph" only exist in perception itself; *it cannot be told*. While Funes's undistracted attention is busy summoning terms, the narrator wishing to transcribe the series must "clear a space" for narration if he wishes to refer the experience—the enumeration of an infinite series—ever so partially. "The main problem here," writes Borges, "is that the enumeration, however partial, of an infinite series, cannot be solved" (AL

164). Overcrowded, unreproduceable series are no different from the overfurnished room in which Proust's narrator cannot find his place: "[I]t was full of things which did not know me, which flung back at me the distrustful glance I cast at them, and, without taking any heed of my existence, showed that I was interrupting the humdrum of theirs" (717).

In Proust, only interference—an *intermittence*—disrupts the unsettling accumulation of objects and makes it manageable. The narrator's grandmother comes into the room "and there opened at once an infinity of space" (718). In a considerably less noble intervention, Carlos Argentino Daneri, the clumsy, despicable owner of the Aleph, intrudes into the narrator's mute contemplation of the infinite universe and opens a similar space. The comparison between the two interruptions is not as gratuitous as it may appear. Proust's crowded room, while challenging, is not entirely unfamiliar or unforeseeable; it corresponds to the nightmarish, overly furnished interiors of the period. On the other hand, in "The Aleph," in order to "clear the space" where the truly unforeseeable, unimaginable universe is represented, a more brutal interruption than that of a *heimlich* grandmother is needed. Daneri's "hated and jovial voice," the disproportionate foolishness of his remark—"Feeling pretty cockeyed, are you, after so much spying into places where you have no business?" (A 28)—provides, through contrast, the only possible interruption.

Heterogeneous Enumeration:
Signaling the Interstice

In Borges, an infinite series can only exist as an illusory translation. Imagined by another (an author Borges has read, one of his own characters), the series is alluded to in the text as fatefully incomplete, fissured by incompetence or forgetfulness. Obviously, it can never be whole, except in the attentive mind of its creator, a fictional character created by Borges. Referring to the universal language proposed by John Wilkins, Borges recalls Wilkins's insistence on analyzing and classifying, elaborating *ab ovo*, in a utopian void, a series of morphological and semantic units "that would organize and contain all human thought" (OI 102). For Wilkins, who devised them, these units are not "stupid arbitrary symbols"; on the contrary, "each word defines itself" (OI 102) and "every letter is meaningful" (OI 103). However, in subsequent readings, the series, no longer upheld by Wilkins's attention, ceases to be an all-meaningful system. Oblivion, accumulated in successive, increasingly distanced readings, will allow the modern reader to domesticate the series differently, to neglect some elements while keeping others, to clear a place. Infinite things, imagined in an alien space— Proust's room, Funes's series, Wilkins's enumerations—suggest to Borges and to the reader the possibility, not only of deleting certain elements but of rescuing others through a renewed, *selective* attention.

Looking over the series of signs that make up the analytical language of John Wilkins, those signs that purport not to be arbitrary, Borges points out "a problem that is impossible or difficult to postpone" (OI 103), that is, the inexplicable choice of the quadragesimal table on which Wilkins's language is based. A necessary choice for Wilkins, it *loses ground* in a modern reading that has only the reader's attention, and not Wilkins's, to uphold it. The perspective of a new reader brings out, instead, the seemingly arbitrary nature of this classification, casting a different light on what now appear to be inane combinations. For example, this bit of nonsense: "Beauty appears in the sixteenth category: it is a viviparous, oblong fish" (OI 103). Signs that wished to be neither awkward nor arbitrary are inevitably so for the reader who is not Wilkins or who is not familiar with the forty categories that make up the series. Mentioned in relation to John Wilkins's classifications, and surely no less arbitrary, are the elements that make up the taxonomy in the Chinese encyclopaedia, or the classifications of the Bibliographical Institute of Brussels, which, in its methods, "also resorts to chaos" (OI 103). Of course, another obvious example of an arbitrary and disturbing series in Borges is the listing of *hrönir* or "secondary objects" of Tlön:

> Curiously, the *hrönir* of second and third degree—the *hrönir* derived from another *hrön*, and those derived from the *hrön* of a *hrön*—exaggerate the aberrations of the initial one; those of the fifth degree are almost uniform; those of the ninth degree become confused with those of the second; in those of the eleventh there is a purity of line not found in the original. The process is cyclical: the *hrön* of twelfth degree begins to fall off in quality. (L 14)

The above series, whether historical, apocryphal, or clearly fictitious, diligently mimic the successive, reasonable itemizing of encyclopaedic classification, the certainty that *a* authoritatively leads to *b*, and *b* to *c*, and that *a, b,* and *c* deserve equal attention. Alphabetic order, here, has the same effect as Proust's "noticing" or Funes's attention, it accounts for enumeration and classification. In his introduction to *The Order of Things*, Foucault comments on the animals listed in the Chinese encyclopedia and reflects on the mock order and minuteness of Borges's series. He finds the items, while startling, clear in themselves and, at first glance, not too disturbing:

> The possibility of dangerous mixtures has been exorcized, heraldry and fable have been relegated to their own exalted peaks: no inconceivable amphibious maidens, no clawed wings, no disgusting, squamous epidermis, none of those polymorphous and demoniacal faces, no creatures breathing fire. The quality of monstrosity here does not affect any real body, nor does it produce modifications of any kind in the bestiary of the imagination; it does not lurk in the depths of any strange power. (xv–xvi)

There is no room here for the scandalous products of an *ars combinatoria* whose horrors Borges has both foreseen and avoided. But while there is no doubt that the lack of common ground for these categories may be disturbing, heterotopia is not the only sign of the monstrosity of Borges's series. No less anomalous, within the enumeration, are some of the categories themselves, less precise than what Foucault implies when he writes that "Each of these strange categories can be assigned a precise meaning and a demonstrable content" (xv). Take, for example, the following segment in the list of animals:

> . . . (f) fabulous ones, (g) stray dogs, (h) those that are included in this classification, (i) those that tremble as if they were mad, (j) innumerable ones, (k) those drawn with a very fine camel's hair brush, (l) etcetera, (m) those that have just broken a flower vase . . . (OI 103)

Both item (l), "etcetera," and item (h), "those that are included in this classification," suggest a subversion that, going beyond what Foucault calls "the interstitial blanks *separating* all these entities from one another" (xvi), devours the mock order of the nonsensical series. As with Tlön's serial *hrönir* of the ninth and the eleventh degree, the categories (h) and (l) in the Chinese encyclopaedia bring to mind the interpolations of Lewis Carroll's tortoise: they infinitely prolong the series and at the same time they clearly suspend it.

Borges presents this example of Chinese taxonomy as an example of the arbitrary classifications of the encyclopedia. One wonders whether a reader might read this series otherwise, in a reading that would go beyond the heterogenous, heterotopic terms that so obviously undo the logic of enumeration. The elements in Borges's series are upheld by alphabetical order. If that order is eliminated and its divisions erased—and if we delete (h) and (l), true flies in the ointment—we read another text, perhaps less heterogeneous, though no less startling. That other text, which would no longer classify and divide (or would do so in a different manner), might go as follows:

> These are animals "that belong to the Emperor: embalmed and trained suckling pigs, mermaids, fantastic stray dogs . . . that tremble as if they were mad and inummerable. Drawn with a very fine camel's hair brush, . . . they are animals that have just broken a vase and from a distance resemble flies.

In this hypothetical text—in which the truly disruptive interpolations (h) and (l) still do not "fit"—heterogeneous elements are grouped according to a different organizing principle, no less reassuring, and no less precarious than an alphabetical sequence. The series in the Chinese encyclopedia, smooth and sequential (smooth because it mimics a sequence) is a mirage of evenly—alphabetically—spaced interstices. The hypothetical text cited above, one of the many texts possible, redistributes the elements in the series and thus redistributes its interstices. It is governed by a different sort of continuity, by Borges's recurring *bête noire*, that is, syntactical continuity. More threatening perhaps than simple enumeration, it does more than accumulate, it actively connects and intertwines; it conjugates, it coordinates, it establishes hierarchies and emphases.

From the very beginning, Borges fights that continuity. For example, in his early "Indagación de la palabra" [Anatomy of the Word], he rebels against the classifying distinctions imposed by syntax: "Representation has no syntax. Can anyone teach me not to confuse the flight of a bird with a bird that flies?" (IA 25). He adds: "The power of syntactical continuity over discourse lies elsewhere. It is the power to shame us into powerlessness, all the while knowing that syntax is nothing. The paradox is profound. Not finding a solution, not being able to find a solution, is a tragedy common to all writing. I accept that tragedy, that treacherous swerving of words . . ." (IA 25).

Borges underlines the difficulty of this necessary acceptance: "May resignation, a virtue to which we must resign ourselves, be with us. This will be our destiny: to get used to syntax, to its treacherous concatenation, to its imprecision; to get used to the "perhaps," and the "buts," and the excessive emphases, to accept deceit and shadow in everything we say" (IA 27). "Going from leaves to birds is easier than from roses to letters" (L 151), thinks Averroes in "Averroes' Search." Going from roses to letters, in spite of the qualitative leap that such a task implies, seems easier for Borges than going from letters to letters.

Concatenation and Betrayal

Discussing various versions of the *regressus in infinitum*, Borges observes that generally the argument "has been used in a negative way" (OI 112). However, he does not dismiss the arguments in its favor, especially Aquinas's cosmological proof:

> The world is an interminable concatenation of causes and each cause is an effect. Each state proceeds from the previous one and determines the following one, but the general series could have *not* existed, since the terms that form it are conditional, that is, fortuitous. Nevertheless, the world *is*; from that fact we can infer a noncontingent first cause, which will be the divinity. This is the cosmological proof; Aristotle and Plato prefigure it; Leibniz rediscovers it. (OI 112)

In the series that Borges offers the reader, the terms are, or seem to be, also fortuitous, but each element does *not* clearly derive from the preceding one and it does *not* determine the following one. Borges's series may also "have *not* existed" and yet they *are*, like the world justified by Aquinas's noncontingent divinity. However, lacking the ordering principle of a noncontingent first cause to give it coherence, Borges's series appears unjustifiable and incongruent.

This incoherence, of course, is relative, since every text, even the most dispersed, most ragged text, must somehow flow sequentially if it is to be read. In Borges, Aquinas's divinity is replaced by a no less inevitable "first cause": the inescapable "treacherous concatenation" of syntax. This "first cause" is less a comfort than a source of "tragedy," since it is both inevitable and contingent. The text sets up a casual concatenation merely justified by its own words, yet what is casual and fortuitous in the series becomes causal at the moment of a reading that is necessarily successive.

Borges's discourse is resigned to the oppression of syntax, resigned to the "treacherous swerving" built into it, which seldom reflects the true will to swerve, to *dissent*, that drives the text. Such resignation may be necessary, but it is less simple than Borges suggests. For acceptance is constantly accompanied by disbelief, the same disbelief vindicated by Borges as "a source of literature" (TE 10). If syntactical concatenation imposes a deficient sequence, Borges's text, even while deferring to that sequence, distrusts and ultimately challenges it. The "verbal objects" linked by Borges are explicitly provisional; they will not be able to destroy the past entirely, in which case there would be no discourse, merely mutilated words like those mentioned by Swift. Instead, they will alter the past by diverging from it, that is, by diverging from previous texts but also from the very words that immediately precede them. In Borges, disbelief leads to the betrayal of a syntactic concatenation that, while not quite abandoned, is always already treacherous.

In "Indagación de la palabra," a half-amused, half-irritated Borges undertakes the mock analysis of a phrase, stopping on every word as if each and all had the same weight, establishing no difference among them beyond that of typographical space. Such an extravagant exercise, applied to the opening sentence of the *Quixote*— *In, a, place*, etc.—is like a caricature, a simple reversal of the Chinese encyclopaedist's taxonomy. If the power of syntax tempts the reader of a deliberately discontinuous enumeration to link all the elements ("Embalmed and trained suckling pigs, mermaids, fantastic stray dogs . . . that tremble as if they were mad and inummerable," etc.), Borges, in the name of that same syntax, breaks up the coherence of Cervantes's phrase—a coherence assured by its very direct style and, more particularly, by a tradition of superstitiously respectful readings that have made the phrase indestructible. The fact that

Borges chooses to apply the artifice of separation to that phrase in particular—a monolithic verbal unit familiar to every Hispanic reader—lays bare a fundamental dissatisfaction followed by an equally fundamental resignation. Cervantes's simple phrase is but a pre-text, allowing for rebellion and final acceptance: after breaking up the phrase, Borges ends up accepting that every term, every mark, is "a promise," "an omen" (IA 10), "a guided word" (IA 11). Syntactical concatenation inevitably faces what is to come.

Time and again, acceptance and disbelief affect the linear, causal conception of syntax. If the word cannot destroy what comes before but only diverge from it, by the same token it cannot face what awaits it in a univocal manner, as in the simple analysis of Cervantes's phrase. Besides, it is evident that any series of words faces a future, a never attainable beyond; no discourse fails to show its incompleteness, to open itself to what has not been said, to what might be added to it. It is hardly necessary to point out Borges's use of this openness in his plots, in the making of his characters and, most especially, in his conception of the literary text as a movable, always incomplete, always open, entity: "I have reflected that it is permissible to see in this 'final' *Quixote* a kind of palimpsest, through which the traces—tenuous but not indecipherable—of our friend's 'previous' writing should be translucently visible. Unfortunately, only a second Pierre Menard, inverting the other's work, would be able to exhume and revive those lost Troys . . ." (L 44). In the future, a second Pierre Menard will invert the work of the first, a new Ryan, in "Theme of the Traitor and the Hero," will continue the writing of a text that already includes him.

There are other ways in which Borges accepts, and at the same time subverts, this open-ended succession. One is, of course, the opening up of the text "in the middle," so obvious in Lewis Carroll's reading of the dialogue between the tortoise and Achilles. A concatenation facing a foreseeable conclusion *z* is derailed by interpolations that redirect it toward other possible conclusions, obliterating the "original" goal. But even the most airtight of series in Borges, the most rigid classifications, question their linear succession. The enumeration of the Chinese taxonomist relies on a comforting alphabetical sequence. Yet even if alphabetical succession is respected and (a) leads to (b), the inclusion of (h) and (l) is as unsettling as the interpolations made by the tortoise, because the chaining of elements, for all its alphabetical rigor, is forced to head *in another direction.* Now if alphabetical classification is put aside and the text is linked according to the traitorous drift of syntax, as was done above, there is still an irreducible gap in the series—the fact that (h) and (l) cannot be incorporated by *any* syntax known to us—and that gap continues to irritate and perplex. Finally, if the series is accepted as is, without questioning the differently graded spaces that may splinter it, its openness to the future is no less clear. The text cancels that future out, turns it circular, and finally neutralizes it: "The alphabet—not to mention the profound circularity it can be given, as the mystical metaphor of 'alpha and omega' testifies—the alphabet is a means of institutionalizing a zero degree of classification."[5]

When considering these impossible series that permanently digress and never achieve their goal, it is worthwhile to take a look at the attitude attributed by Borges to their authors. In Borges, series are always unfinished. If one considers series like those of Funes or John Wilkins that mimic the organization and successive order of an all-encompassing taxonomy, it is obvious that Borges's text could never reproduce them *in extenso.* Instead of attempting that truly unimaginable tautology, Borges, while praising the stammering grandeur or the admirable ingenuity of those series, "quotes" from them in erratic, unpredictable fashion. It is nevertheless curious that in both cases, Funes's catalog of memories and Wilkins's language, Borges, quite fallaciously, projects the unfinished quality of those series, their incompleteness, to a sort of personal weakness—something akin to a moral failing—in their creators. Wilkins and Funes both give up the faith, so to speak. Borges correlates Wilkins's weakness to that of the divinity, as conjectured by Hume: " 'This world . . . is only the first rude essay of some infant deity who afterwards abandoned it, ashamed of his lame performance; it is the work only of some dependent, inferior deity, and is the object of derision to his superiors; it is the production of old age and dotage in some superannuated deity, and ever since his death has run on . . .' " (OI 104). Funes also loses faith in his all-encompassing project; his performance may be judged equally lame. Funes "was dissuaded . . . by two considerations: his awareness that the task was interminable, his awareness that it was useless. He thought that by the hour of his death he would not even have finished classifying all the memories of his childhood" (L 65).

Facing their future, that is, facing the possibility of an endless succession, these series, due to the exhaustion of their makers, are never completed, just as the fragmentary *Quixote* remains unfinished. Pierre Menard does not leave behind a single draft that might prove that his *completed* novel ever existed, no record of the stages of its composition nor of the links that might have joined them, just three fragments: three quotations.

Beyond the Nightmare of Causality

"And yet, and yet—to deny temporal succession, to deny the *I*, to deny the astronomical universe, are apparent desperations and secret assuagements," Borges writes in "New Refutation of Time" (OI 186–87). Borges's systematic unhinging of related elements, his erratic fixation on isolated segments, the fragmentation constantly put into play against predictable sequences, his questioning of the blind belief in a definitive text, all of these must be considered as "apparent desperations and secret assuagements." Borges undermines and disturbs the components of human destiny just as he questions the syntactical configuration of a text. He fears, even exorcizes, the possible reverse of the very heterogeneity he proposes: one subject, one time, one world, one text. "Our destiny," he writes, "is not horrible because of its unreality; it is horrible because it is irreversible and ironbound" (OI 187). To view such unity and univocity as a comfort belongs, as he puts it, to "the province of religion or of tedium" (D 106–7).

If, in "Narrative Art and Magic," Borges proposes an apparently different textual concatenation, he does so without illusions. As might be expected, he disdains the predictable causality of realistic fiction, "attempt[ing] to frame an intricate chain of motives akin to those of real life" (R 37), and instead vindicates the literary causality dictated by "the primitive clarity of magic" (R 37); a causality less primitive and less clear than what the phrase suggests. Borges's interest in the "primitive clarity of magic" has nothing to do with a parade of miracles or a graceless piling up of startling events for the sole purpose of "breaking" with a previous habit of reading. The concatenation suggested by Borges in "Narrative Art and Magic" is of an entirely different sort. It does not reject the wretched causality that we normally attribute to "reality" but neither does it endorse it. On the contrary, it assumes that causality and goes beyond it, in a process of "dangerous connection" (R 38): "[M]agic is not the contradiction of the law of cause and effect but its crown, or nightmare. The miraculous is no less strange in that world than it is in the world of astronomers. All of the laws of nature as well as those of imagination govern it" (R 37).

Because of the diversity of the laws that control it, the falsely predictable, busy causality of magic paradoxically confirms the indeterminacy of Borges's text. It implies the possibility of linking sympathy and distance, exorcism and trust, forcing them into contact. The magic of this art of narrative allows, in one breath, to name the absence of a word and its distant simulacrum, the book and its counterbook. It allows for the adoption of a deviant, uncanny discourse, at home in language yet always estranged.

The description of one of Borges's most memorable moments, as much personal *flânerie* as uncanny derivation, may serve as metaphor for the organization of his text:

> I had spent the afternoon in Barracas, a place I rarely visited, a place whose very *distance* from the scene of my later wanderings gave an *aura of strangeness* to that day. As I had nothing to do in the evening and the weather was fair, I went out after dinner to walk and remember. *I did not wish to have a set destination.* I followed a *random* course, as much as possible; I accepted, with no conscious prejudice other than avoiding the avenues or wide streets, *the most obscure invitations of chance.* But a kind of *familiar gravitation led me away* [una suerte de gravitación familiar me alejó] to certain sections of the city whose names I always wish to remember, for they arouse in me a kind of reverence. I am not speaking of the precise environment of my childhood, my own neighborhood, but of *the still mysterious fringe area beyond it,* which I have possessed completely in words and but little in reality, an area that is familiar and mythological at the same time. The *other side* of the known—its *reverse,* so to speak—are those *penultimate* streets to me, almost as completely hidden as the *buried foundation* of our house or our *invisible* skeleton. (OI 179; my emphasis)

This text, or *fiction* as Borges calls it, was originally titled "Sentirse en muerte," *feeling in death.* It would not be inappropriate to call it *feeling in text,* "sentirse en texto."

Our Invisible Skeleton: The Shape of a Face

Borges's text is fully aware of the fact that "no one exists in any one day, in any one place; no one knows the shape of his face" (OI 8). "Reality," Borges writes, (and he might have said "literature"), "is like our image reflected in all mirrors, a simulacrum that exists only through us, that comes with us, gestures and then leaves us, but that is always there when we search for it" (I 119). Borges knows that in the same way that there is no fixed place for that someone who is no one, no place for the dimensions of his face, there is no fixed place for a text, because "[a] book is not an isolated entity; it is a relation, an axis of innumerable relations" (OI 164). He knows, too, that "literature is not exhaustible, for the simple reason that a single book is not" (OI 164). He knows, finally, that the text is a perpetual *suspension*, something unsaid yet incessantly said, and then incompletely so: that it is "the imminence of a revelation that is not yet produced" (OI 5), a contribution to the "drafts of a book which will lack a final reading" (IA 104).

In "Historia de los ecos de un nombre" [History of the Echoes of a Name], Borges typically brings together three narratives, three instances, one might say, of self-designation. "Separated in time and in space, a god, a fictional character, and a man who is mad and knows it, repeat an obscure statement" (OI 223). At one end is God, asserting "I am Who I am." On the other is the dying Swift, hopelessly mad, repeating "I am what I am, I am what I am." Between the two there is a fiction, Shakespeare's untruthful French soldier in *All's Well That Ends Well*, who succeeds perhaps better than the other two in obliquely naming himself and achieving ephemeral being. Once his ruse is uncovered, Parolles continues to *be* and to *speak* through an imposture that he knows to be false, yet that imposture keeps him going: "Captain I'll be no more; / But I will eat and drink, and sleep as soft / As captain shall: simply the thing I am / Shall make me live." From that tenuous substance, of whose deceptive nature he is well aware, Parolles (whose name is surely no accident), draws his self. With less innocence but with equal fervor, Borges's text chooses the same uncertain foundation to come into being.

Abbreviations of

Works by Borges Cited

in the Text

A   *The Aleph and Other Stories, 1933–1969.* Trans. by Norman Thomas di Giovanni in collaboration with the author. New York: E. P. Dutton, 1970.

AL   *El aleph.* 1949; rpt. Buenos Aires: Emecé, 1963.

D   *Discusión.* 1936; rpt. Buenos Aires: Emecé, 1964.

DR   *Dreamtigers.* Trans. by Mildred Boyer and Harold Morland. Austin: University of Texas Press, 1964.

DB   *Doctor Brodie's Report.* Trans. by Norman Thomas di Giovanni in collaboration with the author. New York: E. P. Dutton, 1978.

EC   *Evaristo Carriego.* Trans. by Norman Thomas di Giovanni with the assistance of Susan Ashe. New York: E. P. Dutton, 1982.

F   *Ficciones.* Ed. Anthony Kerrigan. New York: Grove Press, 1962.

HE   *Historia de la eternidad.* 1936; rpt. Buenos Aires: Emecé, 1965.

I   *Inquisiciones.* Buenos Aires: Proa, 1925.

IA   *El idioma de los argentinos.* Buenos Aires: Gleizer, 1928.

ILI   *Introducción a la literatura inglesa.* Buenos Aires: Columba, 1965.

L   *Labyrinths: Selected Stories and Other Writings.* Ed. Donald Yates and James E. Irby. New York: New Directions, 1964.

MZF   *Manual de zoología fantástica.* Mexico: Fondo de Cultura Económica, 1957.

OI   *Other Inquisitions, 1937–1952.* Trans. by Ruth Simms. Austin: University of Texas Press, 1964.

OI   *Otras inquisiciones.* 1952; rpt. Buenos Aires: Emecé, 1962.

OP   *Obra poética (1923–1966).* Buenos Aires: Emecé, 1966.

R   *Borges: A Reader. A Selection from the Writings of Jorge Luis Borges.* Ed. Emir Rodríguez Monegal and Alastair Reid. New York: E. P. Dutton, 1981.

SP   *Selected Poems, 1923–1967.* Ed. Norman Thomas Di Giovanni. New York: Penguin, 1985.

TE   *El tamaño de mi esperanza.* Buenos Aires: Proa, 1926.

UHI   *A Universal History of Infamy.* Trans. by Norman Thomas di Giovanni. New York: E. P. Dutton, 1972.

Notes

1 Shadow Plays

1. For titles of Borges's books cited in the text, see the preceding list of abbreviations. We have used existing English translations in most cases, making minor alterations when we considered that the English version did not adequately illustrate the point made in the original. All other translations are our own, unless otherwise specified.

2. Ernesto Sábato, "Borges," *Uno y el universo* (Buenos Aires: Sudamericana, 1968): 21–26.

3. Nathaniel Hawthorne, "Wakefield," *Twice Told Tales* (Boston: James R. Osgood and Company, 1878): 158. Further references appear directly in the text.

4. Adolfo Bioy Casares, *La invención de Morel*, prólogo de Jorge Luis Borges (Buenos Aires: Losada, 1949). Borges restates his argument some years later when he writes that in the short story "each detail exists as a function of the general plot; such rigorous correspodence may be necessary and admirable in a brief text, but would be tedious in a novel, a genre that in order to avoid appearing too artificial or mechanical requires the discreet inclusion of independent traits" ("La última invención de Hugh Walpole," *La Nación*, February 10, 1943).

5. Richard Burgin, *Conversations with Jorge Luis Borges* (New York: Avon, 1970): 31. Further references appear directly in the text.

6. References to Joseph von Sternberg, so frequent in the early Borges, deserve to be considered more attentively than they are here. Two quotations from von Sternberg, echoing Borges's aesthetics in *A Universal History of Infamy*, are of interest. Referring to *The Salvation Hunters* (1924), he writes: "I had in mind a visual poem. . . . Instead of scenery which meant nothing, an emotionalized background that would transfer itself into my foreground" (*Fun in a Chinese Laundry* [New York: Macmillan, 1965]: 202). Discussing his last film, *Anatahan* (1954), von Sternberg states: "[I]f I did not work on location, it was on purpose . . . I recreated China in a studio for *Shanghai Express*, for *The Shanghai Gesture*, for *Macao*. . . . Everything is artificial in *Anatahan*, even the clouds are painted and the plane is a toy. This film is my own creation. To reality, one should prefer the *illusion of reality*" (Herman Weinberg, *Joseph von Sternberg* [New York: Dutton, 1967]: 125).

7. Borges, speaking of Scott Fitzgerald: "He was always on the surface of things, no? After all, why shouldn't you, no?" (Burgin 21).

8. Silvina Ocampo, "Images de Borges," *L'Herne*, Paris: 1964: 27.

9. "Sobre la descripción literaria," *Sur* 97 (1942): 101.

10. Roger Caillois, "Postface du traducteur," in Jorge Luis Borges, *Histoire de l'infamie/Histoire de l'éternité* (Paris: Union générale des éditions, 1964): 292–93.

11. "Overwhelmingly, endlessly, Orson Welles shows fragments of the life of Charles Foster Kane and invites us to combine them and to reconstruct him. Multiplicity and disconnection abound in this film" ("An Overwhelming Film," in Edgardo Cozarinsky, *Borges in/and/on/Film*, trans. Gloria Waldman and Ronald Christ [New York: Lumen Books, 1988]: 55). Further references appear directly in the text.

2　Textual Rubrications

1. James E. Irby, "Encuentro con Borges," in James E. Irby, Napoléon Murat, and Carlos Peralta, eds., *Encuentro con Borges* (Buenos Aires: Galerna, 1968): 37.

2. Jean Wahl, "Les personnes et l'impersonnel," *L'Herne* (Paris: 1964): 258.

3. Maurice Blanchot, *Le livre à venir* (Paris: Gallimard, 1959): 163.

4. Michel Foucault, *The Order of Things: An Archeology of the Human Sciences* (New York: Vintage, 1970): xvii.

5. Tzvetan Todorov, *The Poetics of Prose*, trans. Richard Howard (Ithaca: Cornell University Press, 1977): 74.

3 Fragments and Greeds

1. Nathalie Sarraute, "Ce que je cherche à faire," *Nouveau roman: hier, aujourd'hui*, vol. 2 (Paris: Union générale d'éditions, 1972): 26. See also Gérard Genette: "[T]he contemporary novel . . . does not hesitate to establish between narrator and character(s) a variable or floating relationship, a pronominal vertigo in tune with a freer logic and a more complex conception of 'personality'. . . . The Borgesian fantastic, in this respect emblematic of a whole modern literature, does *not accept person*" (*Narrative Discourse: An Essay in Method*, trans. Jane E. Lewin [Ithaca: Cornell University Press, 1980]: 246–47).

2. Hans Magnus Enzensberger, "Estructuras topológicas de la literatura moderna," *Sur* 300 (1966): 15.

4 Postulating a Reality, Selecting a Reality

1. Jacques Lacan, "Seminar on 'The Purloined Letter,'" *French Freud, Yale French Studies* 48 (1972): 50.

2. Robert Louis Stevenson, "Memories and Portraits," *The Works of Robert Louis Stevenson*, vol. 6 (New York: Bigelow, Brown and Co., 1908): 128. Further references appear directly in the text.

3. Roland Barthes, "The Reality Effect," *The Rustle of Language*, trans. Richard Howard (New York: Hill and Wang, 1986): 141–48.

4. Henry James, Preface to *The Spoils of Poynton*, in *The Future of the Novel* (New York: Vintage, 1956): 52.

5. José Hernández, *El gaucho Martín Fierro / The Gaucho Martin Fierro*, bilingual edition, English version by C. E. Ward (Albany, N.Y.: SUNY Press, 1967): 237.

6. Jorge Luis Borges, *Oeuvre poétique* (Paris: Gallimard, 1970): 7.

7. Georges Charbonnier, *Entretiens avec Jorge Luis Borges* (Paris: Gallimard, 1967): 120, 128.

8. Henry James, "The Art of Fiction," in *The Future of the Novel* (New York: Vintage, 1956): 23.

5 Converting the Simulacrum

1. Sigmund Freud, "The 'Uncanny,'" *On Creativity and the Unconscious* (New York: Harper Colophon Books, 1958): 129. Further references appear directly in the text.

2. Marcial Tamayo and Adolfo Ruiz Díaz, *Borges: Enigma y clave* (Buenos Aires: Nuestro Tiempo, 1955): 63.

3. Marcel Schwob, *Vies imaginaires* (Paris: Gallimard, 1957): 10.

6 Pleasure and Perplexity

1. Michel Foucault, *The Order of Things* (New York: Vintage Books, 1973): xvi. Further references appear directly in the text.

2. "La personalidad y el Buddha," *Sur* 192–94 (1950): 34.

3. Etiemble, "Un homme à tuer: Jorge Luis Borges, cosmopolite," *Littérature dégagée (1942–1953)* (Paris: Gallimard, 1955): 133.

4. I quote from the first English interview with Borges:

> *Interviewer*: Do you expect many people who read your work to catch the allusions and references?
> *Borges*: No. Most of those allusions and references are merely put there as a kind of private joke.
> *I*: A *private* joke?
> *B*: A joke not to be shared with other people. I mean, if they share it, all the better; but if they don't, I don't care a hang about it.
> *I*: Then it's the opposite approach to allusion from, say, Eliot in *The Waste Land*.
> *B*: I think that Eliot and Joyce wanted their readers to be rather mystified and so to be worrying out the sense of what they had done. (Ronald Christ, "The Art of Fiction," *The Paris Review* 40 [1967]: 151)

5. Marcial Tamayo and Adolfo Ruiz Díaz, *Borges: Enigma y clave* (Buenos Aires: Nuestro Tiempo, 1955): 17.

6. Maurice Blanchot, *The Gaze of Orpheus and Other Literary Essays*, ed. P. Adams Sitney, trans. Lydia Davis (Barrytown, N.Y.: Station Hill Press, 1981): 105. Further references appear directly in the text.

7. Bertolt Brecht, "Alienation Effects in the Narrative Pictures of the Elder Breughel," *Brecht on Theatre: The Development of an Aesthetic* (New York: Hill and Wang, 1964): 157.

8. "Alienation Effects on Chinese Acting," *Brecht on Theatre*: 94.

7 The Buried Foundation

1. Jorge Luis Borges, "Sobre la descripción literaria," *Sur* 97 (1942): 101.

2. James E. Irby, "Encuentro con Borges," in James E. Irby, Napoléon

Murat, and Carlos Peralta, eds., *Encuentro con Borges* (Buenos Aires: Galerna, 1968): 28–29.

3. Leslie Stephen, "A Critical Essay on Robert Louis Stevenson," *The Works of Robert Louis Stevenson*, vol. 9 (New York: Bigelow, Brown and Co., 1908): 6.

4. Marcel Proust, *Remembrance of Things Past*, vol. 1, trans. Scott Moncrieff and Terence Kilmartin (New York: Random House, 1981): 100. Further references appear directly in the text.

5. Roland Barthes, *Critical Essays*, trans. Richard Howard (Evanston: Northwestern University Press, 1972): 176.

Index

About the Authors

Sylvia Molloy is Albert Schweitzer Professor in the Humanities at New York University. Her work includes *La Diffusion de la littérature hispano-américaine en France* (1972), *Las letras de Borges* (1979), *At Face Value: Autobiographical Writing in Spanish America* (1990), and many articles on Latin American literature and culture. Her novel, *En breve cárcel* (1981), has been translated into English as *Certificate of Absence* (1989). She is currently working on a book on the construction of gender and gender deviance in connection with notions of national selfhood in turn-of-the-century Latin America.

Oscar Montero is Professor of Spanish American Literature at Lehman College and the Graduate Center of the City University of New York. He is the author of *The Name Game: Writing/Fading Writer in "De donde son los cantantes"* (1988) and *Erotismo y representación en Julián del Casal* (1993).